Praise

This book squarely fits into my area of expertise. The playground I play in is "Coaches Who've Created a Job, Not a Business." *The Coaching Blueprint* is a quick and powerful read as the "fluff" many authors fill their books with is not in this one. It's direct, to the point, and filled with powerful ideas you can immediately implement. I highly recommend it.

–Mitchell Levy, Global Credibility Expert

"It's not just a book; it's a transformative guide for anyone seeking to make a genuine impact in the world of coaching. With its rich tapestry of wisdom, this book is a must-read for both novice and experienced coaches alike."

–Jason Miller

Tony DUrso has a voice that resonates with millions. As the *Tony DUrso Show host*, he's enjoyed a flourishing career, boasting over 38 million listens and downloads in his seven-year journey. But behind every great voice is the power of great words, and for Tony, those words were crafted by Kara James.

Tony candidly shares, "When people say they're good at content, I'm usually skeptical. What does that even mean?" But when he worked with Kara, the difference was clear. "She's not just good; she's exceptional."

Showcasing the work Kara did for him, Tony points to his Twitter page. "See this? 'Come for the knowledge, stay for the inspiration.' That's Kara's magic." And it's not just Twitter. Kara's touch can be felt across Tony's digital presence. Her word wizardry is evident, whether it's the catchy phrases on his website or the compelling banner texts on his LinkedIn and Instagram.

And Tony is particularly proud of one piece of content. "Look at my grow page," he beams, "That tagline: 'Want massive engagement on your podcasts and social media? It's what we do.' That's all Kara."

Summing up his experience, Tony, with the charm of his Italian-Chicago roots, heartily recommends, "If you need the right words, and trust me, words matter—go straight to Kara James. She's a maestro in the world of content. Thanks a ton, Kara!"

–Tony DUrso

The Coach's Blueprint

Strategies, Tips, and Secrets for Impactful Success

KARA JAMES

ISBN: 979-8-89079-074-3 (Paperback)
ISBN: 979-8-89079-075-0 (Ebook)

Table of Contents

Case Studies

Amanda Maney's Transformative Experience with Coach Kara James

In the coaching field, a coach's impact on their client depends on how they go about it. Amanda Maney received coaching from Kara James, and it was a life-changing experience for her. Amanda puts it this way: "When I think about Kara, three things stand out. She's warm, super smart, and totally gets me."

Amanda was impressed by how kind and caring Kara is. "She's professional but also very empathetic. When I was feeling unsure, her kind words made a big difference. It felt like our relationship was more than just business."

Amanda also pointed out how insightful Kara is. "She's good at understanding what I'm saying, thinking it over, and then summing it up in a way that opens my eyes. Every session feels like a journey where I discover something new. She didn't just guide me; she changed how I see things, showing me options I hadn't thought about."

However, what stood out for Amanda was Kara's ability to adapt. "Kara is awesome at adjusting her coaching to fit who I am and what I've been through. I've had coaches who didn't get that before, so Kara's approach felt empowering."

Amanda's changes weren't just about her career; they were personal, too. She wraps it up by saying, "Every step forward I take in my coaching business, I owe a lot to Kara. She's helped me grow in my job and as a person. To Kara: You've made a huge difference in my life. Thank you."

–Amanda Maney

A Closer Look at James Foo Torres' Experience with Kara

James Foo Torres had some great things to say about working with Kara. He thinks she's super helpful when it comes to business advice, especially when it comes to crafting compelling messages for customers and figuring out how to attract people to a business without spending loads on advertising.

He says, "Kara is an amazing resource if you need help with messaging, irresistible offer creation, and building a business with organic traffic." This is a big deal because, in the world of business, getting your message right and attracting customers without a big advertising budget can be tough. James believes that Kara has the know-how to make it happen.

It's not just about business. James mentioned that chatting with Kara is always nice. He adds, "She is also a lovely human being you can always have a pleasant conversation with." That's important because nobody wants to work with someone who's all business and no fun, right?

If you're considering starting a business or trying to grow one, James suggests contacting Kara. After all, it's always good to have someone experienced to guide you along the way.

–James Foo Torres

Colton Pomeroy: A Skeptic Turned Believer with Kara's Coaching

Colton Pomeroy knows his way around the coaching world. So, when he came across Kara's program, he thought, *What could this offer that I don't already know?* However, taking a leap of faith with Kara turned out to be a decision he'd never regret.

"I thought I had seen it all in coaching," Colton shares, "but Kara's course was a complete game-changer." From building a strong coaching program to attracting more clients, Kara's strategies were fresh and effective. "It wasn't just theory," Colton recalls, "I could actually use what I learned."

The results spoke for themselves. Colton beams, "In no time, I added forty new clients! My business just kept growing."

Colton has a message for those unsure about joining Kara's course: "Don't let doubt hold you back. Kara's Coaches Offer Collective course is a goldmine. It transformed my business, and I'm sure it'll do wonders for yours, too."

–Colton Pomeroy

Joel's Journey with Kara James from Pursue and Thrive

Joel wanted to get more people interested in his business. That's when he found Kara James from Pursue and Thrive. Joel says, "Kara knows how to make things clear and help businesses grow."

Working with Kara was a game-changer for Joel. He shares, "She showed me how to attract more customers the right way. Every idea she gave just made a lot of sense."

What stood out to Joel was how practical Kara's advice was. "She gave clear steps and plans," Joel adds, "Everything was easy to follow and made a big difference."

Looking back, Joel feels he made the right choice. "If you want to grow your business and get good advice, talk to Kara. She really helped me out."

–Joel Phillips

Mieke Vander Heyden: Growing Online with Kara's Help

Mieke is a psychotherapist and wanted to reach more people online. She teamed up with Kara and her online learning site. Mieke says, "Kara's site is full of helpful stuff that made planning so much easier."

Mieke loved the personal touch with Kara. She recalls, "Kara is kind and really listens. She helped me feel confident about going online."

What Mieke found special was Kara's way of teaching. "Every session with Kara felt like a new discovery," Mieke notes, "She showed me things I hadn't even thought of."

Mieke's thankful for the growth she's experienced. She shares, "Kara's help was more than just business; it felt personal. Big thanks to Kara for everything!"

–Mieke Vander Heyden

Nicole Gwanzura: Finding Value with Kara's Guidance

Nicole had offers for her company but felt something was missing. She asked Kara for help. Nicole says, "Kara showed me what was valuable in my offers."

Nicole was amazed by Kara's ability to listen and advise. She recalls, "Every time we talked, she gave advice that took my offers up a notch. It was always clear and helpful."

What Nicole appreciated most was Kara's practicality. "Kara gave steps that were easy to follow," Nicole shares, "They made a big difference."

Summing up her experience, Nicole says, "I'd tell anyone in any business to go to Kara for advice. She really knows her stuff."

–Nicole Gwanzura

Sutton McCraney: Discovering the Personal Touch in Business Coaching with Kara

Embarking on the journey of business can be daunting. Navigating through challenges, brainstorming ideas, and seeking validation for one's strategies can often feel overwhelming. Sutton McCraney, a dedicated professional, recognized this when he sought out a business coach. That's when she encountered Kara.

From their first interaction, Sutton found that Kara exuded warmth and had a profound knowledge of her field. "Conversations with Kara never felt like typical business discussions. There was always a blend of professionalism with a touch of genuine care," Sutton recalls.

What struck Sutton most profoundly was Kara's ability to listen. In an era where everyone is eager to give their two cents, finding someone who genuinely wants to hear your ideas is invaluable. "Kara was that sounding board I desperately needed. Whenever I presented an idea, she would dissect it, appreciate its merits, and gently offer ways to refine it," she says.

One thing Sutton didn't expect was how swiftly time would pass during their sessions. She adds, "It wasn't just about the business aspect. Kara truly wanted to understand my vision and passions and align her advice with them. It's rare to find a coach who immerses themselves into your world like Kara does."

The evidence of Kara's commitment to her profession is clear not only through her vast knowledge but also in the palpable passion she exhibits. Sutton could feel how much she loved what she did and how deeply she cared for her clients.

In wrapping up her reflection on her time with Kara, Sutton gives her recommendation without hesitation: "The world of business coaching is vast, but if you're looking for someone who brings a wealth of experience paired with a genuine personal touch, Kara is the one to turn to."

–Sutton McCraney

Paty Mariposa: A Flourishing Membership Site with Kara's Insight

Navigating the online world, especially in the domain of membership websites, can be quite a challenge. Paty Mariposa and her business partner understood the stakes and diligently offered their members the best experience. When they met with Kara for a complimentary review of their membership website, Mariposas Kaleidoscope Tribe, they weren't sure what to expect.

From the onset, Kara recognized the potential and value embedded in their service. "She acknowledged our efforts and showed genuine appreciation for the resource we had built," Paty recalls. Yet, Kara's feedback wasn't only praising. She followed up with actionable tips that resonated with Paty and her partner.

"We were given a roadmap of sorts," Paty says, reflecting on the meeting. These weren't just generic pointers but tailored suggestions directly relevant to their platform. Armed with this newfound knowledge, the duo immediately incorporated Kara's insights into their website.

For many, the true measure of a consultant's worth isn't just in the feedback they give but in the tangible results that follow. Paty and her partner are filled with anticipation, eager to see how these changes will spur growth for Mariposas Kaleidoscope Tribe.

In reflecting on the experience, Paty states, "Guidance is crucial in the business realm. When that guidance is validating and actionable, as it was with Kara, it can be a game-changer."

–Paty Mariposa

Anna Marie Ramirez: Crafting the Perfect Offer with Kara James

When crafting an offer, it's not always about the big changes. Sometimes, the devil is in the details. Anna Marie Ramirez recognized this when she contacted Kara James, hoping to refine her business proposal.

Anna had a clear aim: to make her new offer not just good but irresistibly appealing to her clientele. Kara was her chosen ally in this mission. "From our initial conversation, she delved deep, providing a thoughtful review of my existing offer," Anna recalls. The result wasn't just a list of suggestions but a detailed strategy that illuminated the path ahead.

One aspect that Anna found particularly impressive was Kara's communication skills. "She didn't just hand over feedback; she communicated it clearly and easily," Anna mentions. It wasn't a one-and-done deal. As Anna provided more context, Kara continuously enriched her suggestions, adding layers of value to the proposal.

Anna's experience speaks to Kara's dedication and expertise. "In a world where many professionals provide surface-level advice, Kara stands out with her depth and genuine commitment to value addition," Anna opines.

Ending on a note of gratitude and endorsement, Anna shares, "If you're aiming for excellence and need someone to guide you there, Kara's the one to turn to. Her insights have been invaluable to me."

–Anna Marie Ramirez

Sarah Vermazen: From Solitude to Strategy with Kara James

Embarking on an entrepreneurial journey can often be a solitary endeavor. Sarah Vermazen can vouch for this, having experienced the highs and lows of setting up her business. However, there was a guiding star in her path: Kara James.

Sarah's story with Kara isn't about a one-time consultation. It's a series of engagements, each offering a step toward clarity. "I often turned to Kara to discuss my business progress," Sarah shares. "Every time, she was this calming presence, someone who genuinely cared and motivated me."

What stood out for Sarah was Kara's innate ability to empathize. "It's not just about the business side of things; it's the emotional journey, too," Sarah muses. "Starting a business is like unveiling a piece of your soul, and when doubts crept in, Kara was there, understanding my phase and journey."

Sarah's journey wasn't without its fair share of ideas. However, for every thought, there was a myriad of questions. Kara, with her trove of resources, had the answers. "It felt like she had this magical collection of sheets for every business need. Kara would simply respond with every strategic query I had, 'I have a sheet for that.' It was comforting, to say the least."

Sarah's experience culminates in a heartfelt recommendation. "Being an entrepreneur can sometimes feel lonely, but you're never alone with Kara. Whether for strategy or a motivational push, I'd tell anyone to reach out to Kara. She's truly been a beacon of guidance for me."

–Sarah Vermazen

Annette Berry: Thriving Online with Kara James' Expertise

Annette Berry is all about health and fitness, coaching people online to be their best. However, when it came to setting up her online tools, she turned to Kara James for some expert advice. Annette recalls, "I had ideas, but Kara brought them to life in ways I hadn't imagined."

One of the major boosts for Annette's business was the setup of her Linktree and social media landing page. "Kara connected everything smoothly," Annette shares. "It made reaching my clients through emails so much easier. My business started growing like never before."

What Annette loved most was Kara's dedication. She wasn't just a once-off helper. Annette notes, "Even after our main tasks were done, Kara was just an email away. Whenever I had questions or faced a problem, she was there to help."

Wrapping up her thoughts, Annette has a clear recommendation. "If you want your business to shine online, you need someone like Kara. She's a powerhouse in her field, giving my business a massive boost. Big thanks and thumbs up to Kara James!"

–Annette Berry

Introduction

The Coach's Blueprint: Strategies, Tips, and Secrets for Impactful Success isn't just another business book; it's a compass guiding you through the maze of coaching and entrepreneurship. It's shaped by my years of experience, fine-tuned to provide you with tangible insights.

Coaching, to me, is more than just a career. It's the delicate art of fostering growth and guiding transformations. As you read this book, think of it as us sitting across from each other in a quiet office, exchanging stories, strategies, and visions for the future. As I wrote it, that's what I envisioned—a heartfelt conversation between me and a close friend who wanted to know the good and the bad and how to rise above all the noise and stand out and succeed in a crowded market.

In my coaching business, Pursue and Thrive, it's all about creating room for genuine growth. At Pursue and Thrive, your journey takes center stage. As an entrepreneur seeking to transform your offers from lackluster to irresistible, I'm here to guide you with a track record that speaks for itself. Together, we'll weave crystal-clear messaging that captures attention and drives those coveted high conversion rates.

As you navigate the complex business landscape, rest assured that I'm no stranger to strategic leadership. Holding the reins as a board member within the esteemed Strategic Advisor Board, I'm part of a dream team of ten that's dedicated to elevating your success.

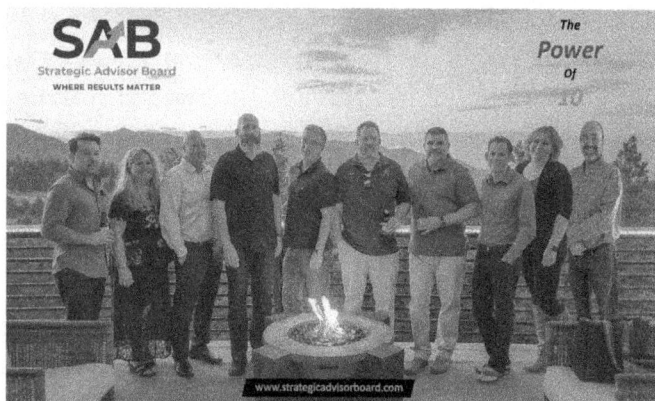

Our Strategic Advisor Board isn't just a name; it's a global powerhouse in management consulting. Our expertise lies in fostering game-changing partnerships for small and mid-tier businesses, equipping you with the strategies and resources needed to clinch those transformative alliances.

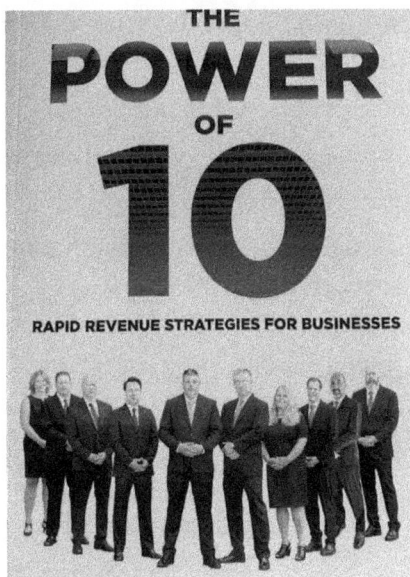

With our wide-reaching network, you'll effortlessly tap into new markets and growth opportunities.

In addition to my vast experience, I am a certified retreat host through Retreat Boss. This accreditation enables me to host immersive retreats seamlessly and beautifully, providing an unparalleled experience for my clients.

Let me bring my expertise to the table, honed through dual roles:

- Guiding startups toward success
- Crafting irresistible offers

- Ensuring messages resonate with your target market
- Creating captivating sales pages
- Pioneering organic traffic strategies
- Mastering focus and organization
- Building bridges as an influencer/affiliate connector
- Connecting fellow business owners for mutual growth

Notable Accomplishments

- Earned HarvardX certification in productivity, a testament to my commitment to peak efficiency.
- Certified in 2020 as a "triple threat" digital marketer specializing in copywriting, irresistible offers, and high-converting funnels.
- Featured in *Forbes Magazine* and *Business Insider* and graced the pages of *PIVOT Magazine* thrice.
- Named among *Brainz's* top 500 entrepreneurs in 2020, sharing company with luminaries like Kamala Harris and Elon Musk.

When I'm not with clients, I enjoy life in the serene Finger Lakes Region of Upstate New York, as a married mom of three remarkable adults.

Discover more:
Pursue and Thrive, LLC (https://www.pursueand-thrive.com)
Strategic Advisor Board (https://www.strategicadvi-sorboard.com)

While we offer many coaching programs and offers, the most comprehensive program that will take any coach from startup to successful scaling is our twelve-month program:

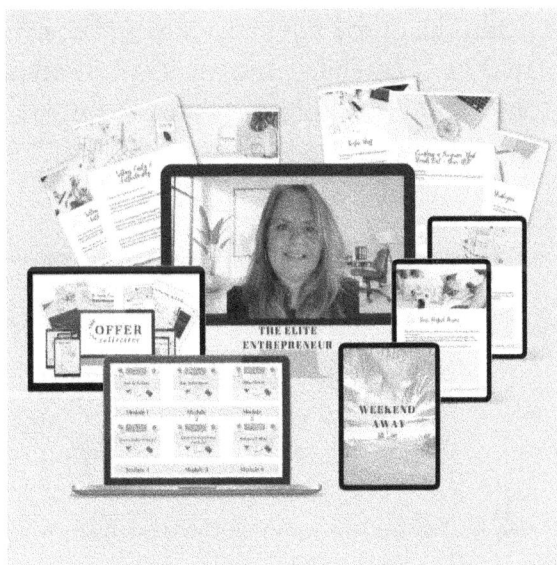

The Elite Entrepreneur

Embrace a transformative year meticulously shaped to amplify your coaching status and personally ensure consistent revenue. This program will take you from startup to successfully scaling with ease.

You will become THE only choice in your field.

Go to the website below to learn more about this incredible one-on-one, twelve-month hybrid experience: https://pursueandthrive.com/elite-entrepreneur

If you're fueled by ambition to elevate and distinctively position your coaching brand as THE go-to expert in your field, The Elite Entrepreneur hybrid coaching is more than just a coaching program; it's your compass—your north star—guiding you toward unparalleled coaching mastery. Dive in and get started today.

While the journey to coaching excellence involves mastering many strategies and processes, it's equally about personal evolution. You'll want to keep growing and learning and, most importantly, stay true to your authentic self. The impact you wish to create in others begins with the changes you embrace within. Together, we position you as the leader you were meant to be.

For now, let's get your business transformation started with this coaching blueprint.

This book is truly about you. As you delve into its chapters, envision it as a roadmap filled with shared wisdom, insights, and guiding principles.

By the end, I hope you have a richer understanding of what is needed to elevate your coaching business.

Are you ready to get started on our journey together? Let's go!

CHAPTER 1

The Octagon of Business Success

Much like a finely crafted clock, business thrives on intricate systems working seamlessly together. Each cog and wheel, no matter how small, is essential to the clock ticking harmoniously. Similarly, a successful coaching business thrives on eight essential processes, each crucial for operating effectively. Miss one, and it's the broken link.

1. **Client Acquisition:** On the surface, this might seem like merely seeking out potential clients. However, beneath it is a deeper art. It's not just about finding them but magnetically drawing them in. What's the emotional messaging your business tells? Does it speak to your ideal client's pain or desires and aspirations? The nuances in this process can be elusive, and an experienced guide can help unearth hidden insights.

1

We'll discuss a lot about messaging and its importance in Chapter 3.

2. **Sales Process:** Conversion isn't solely a numbers game; it's about connection, which this book will discuss extensively. Connecting with your audience is key to a thriving business. This delicate art guides potential clients from a flicker of interest to a burning commitment. Beyond just having a procedure, it's the genuine and authentic touchpoints that provide balance.

   It's said that the average touch point to get a cold lead to a buying customer is now forty-seven. That means a stranger must see your video or social media posts forty-seven times (give or take) to feel they know, like, and trust you.

3. **Customer Onboarding:** This is where the seeds of a lasting relationship are planted. Beyond creating a positive first impression, it's a nuanced dance of setting expectations, sparking excitement, and cementing trust. The journey's trajectory can be influenced significantly by this stage.

   I know this firsthand. In the early years, I would pay to be a part of giveaways and build my email list by having leads opt in for my gift in exchange for their email, and what did I do then? I didn't follow up and nurture properly, so when I decided to send an email, they had no idea who I was. You need to remember that people are inundated with emails and DMs. If you're not in their inbox regularly or posting nearly every day, they most likely won't remember you and will either unsubscribe from your email list or delete your emails without opening them.

4. **Customer Support Process:** Beyond problem-solving, it's about the emotional journey you guide your clients through. Is their journey with you merely transactional, or is it built on a foundation of valued relationships? The path chosen here can be the difference between a fleeting client and a lifelong client who repeatedly buys from and refers people to your business.

My son used to sell an amazing green powder for morning smoothies that was delicious and super nutritious. The company had exploded quickly and was even featured on one of the morning TV shows. However, their fulfillment process was horrible. They could never get it right. It was a monthly subscription and would either be late or not show up at all. This was happening to my sisters-in-law, my son, and me. Although their customer service representatives were kind when you reached someone, they couldn't keep up with all the issues. This left customers frustrated and wondering when their product would arrive and angry because they hadn't received a return email for days. I emailed the CEO and offered our advisory board services because I wanted to see this company succeed, but I never heard back. I'm unsure if they're still in business, but I know I'll never buy from them again.

5. **Communication Process:** Beyond mere words, this is about the essence your business exudes. Does it speak with clarity, warmth, and genuineness? Crafting this voice is not just essential; it's imperative.

   There's a fine line between boundaries and being there for your clients. You'll want to set these expectations in place from the beginning of your coaching and have it in writing. I offer "unlimited" Voxer service for my VIP clients, and it goes without saying that I'm not available in the evenings after 7:00 or on weekends unless something is happening with the client, for example, a launch. So far, my time has been respected, but if I did have someone reach out during off hours with simple questions, I'd be sure to get something on paper so everyone was on the same page.

6. **Fulfillment:** Delivery isn't just about meeting expectations; it's about surpassing them. More than just a service, the unseen details, the extra mile, leave an indelible mark.

   I love it when there is a simple handwritten "thank you" when I order a book or gift. It only takes several seconds, but that warm thought I have for that business makes me choose them the next time.

7. **Referral Process:** How does one channel goodwill into tangible results? It's in the art of turning satisfied clients into vocal advocates, crafting experiences they want to shout about from the rooftops. Always under-promise and over-deliver.

I love it when I invest in a program and don't know exactly what is in it; I just know it will help me get from A to B. For example, I purchased an Instagram reels course full of so many helpful nuggets that I didn't find out about until I got it. What a pleasant surprise! I told my network about it. So, not only did she get a lot more sales, but do you think we'll want to buy something from this person again if she offers another course for a different platform? You betcha! She gained a village of raving, referring customers.

Automated Business Blueprint

ATTRACT TRAFFIC → CAPTURE LEADS → NURTURE RELATIONSHIP → CONVERT TO CASH → DELIVER & WOW → LIFETIME CUSTOMER → SPREAD THE LOVE

8. **Internal and External Processes:** The smooth running of the business machinery often remains unseen yet is crucial. This is where we see a lot of hidden fraction points and bottlenecks. Often, an external perspective can spotlight areas we become blind to.

   You may have heard that the business owner is usually so far up in their jar they can't read their label. Having a fresh pair of eyes on the processes always helps.

This is how your process should be set up:

As you can see, each pillar, in its own right, is a universe of intricacies and details.

For instance:

Client Acquisition is not just about finding clients but aligning your service to their core needs, desires, and aspirations.

The **Sales Process** isn't just a sequence of steps; it's an art that requires understanding psychological triggers, trust-building, and timing.

Customer Onboarding isn't a mere introduction; it's the first chapter of your client's journey with you. How you set the tone here can make or break their experience.

While this book offers a preliminary guide to these pillars, achieving true mastery involves going much deeper. It requires tailored strategies, personalized feedback, and, most importantly, guidance through each stage.

How committed are you to unlocking these pillars' full potential for your business?

I've added tips, secrets, gold nuggets, and fun facts that I think you'll find helpful.

Tip: Infuse gamification into your coaching program. Transforming progress into a game with badges, points, or rewards can spike client motivation and engagement. In this day and age, where up-and-coming professionals have grown up in a gaming world, this has become increasingly popular.

Secret: One secret to running a successful coaching business is identifying and mastering the micro-processes within each pillar. For instance, within the "Customer Relations" pillar, understanding client behavior and feedback loops could be a game-changer. When you get granular with each pillar, you're no longer skimming the surface; you're diving deep, and that's where those gaps, holes, and bottlenecks are.

Gold Nugget #1: Introduce the concept of 'Random Inspiration Days.' These are days when you delve into a subject completely unrelated to coaching. The cross-pollination of ideas can be a game-changer.

Gold Nugget #2: Don't try to master all the pillars at once or try to do it by yourself. You will miss things. You don't know what you don't know.

Gold Nugget #3: Consistency is a superpower. While exploring the eight pillars, maintaining a consistent approach across all dimensions ensures a steady progression. Avoid hopping from one strategy to another without giving the first ample time to yield results. You'll never know what works and what doesn't if you jump quickly from one strategy to the next.

Fun Fact #1: Did you know that some of the most renowned coaches in history didn't start in the profession? Many transitioned from diverse careers like teaching, sports, or even acting.

Fun Fact #2: The oldest client relationship might be from the culinary world. Ancient Romans had their favorite street food vendors, returning to them repeatedly—an early form of client retention.

Summary:

You discovered the eight critical business processes that stand at the core of every successful coaching business, offering a foundation for lasting success.

If you'd like to have these eight processes set up and smoothly running in your business, join us in The Elite Entrepreneur. https://pursueandthrive.com/elite-entrepreneur

Action Points:

1. List the eight pillars and give yourself a score from 1-10 (1 being lowest). Where are you currently in your business?

2. Reflect on which pillar you believe is your strongest and which needs the most attention.
3. Create a monthly plan to improve one pillar at a time.

CHAPTER 2

Crafting Compelling Offers that Convert

In the ever-evolving world of coaching, where every conversation can ignite change, the heart of your offers should reflect a deep understanding of your audience's aspirations, needs, and desires. This is what distinguishes a passing glance from a dedicated, purposeful commitment. Let's unravel the method behind constructing coaching offers that are a no-brainer and have your ideal client saying, "I'm in!"

The Anatomy of an Irresistible Offer

An impactful coaching offer is more than a list of services. As the saying goes, "No one wants your course." They only care about the transformation you will help them get, whether it's creating a successful business, finding the love of their life, or getting in shape. Envision your offer as a vehicle, taking your clients from their current state (point A) to their desired future (point B). This doesn't have to be complicated. As a matter of fact, it should not be. It should be as simple and quick as possible, but it must be transformative.

Take Amanda, a skilled life coach. Recognizing the challenge of her clients—managing demanding careers alongside personal lives—she curated an offer that wasn't just about coaching sessions. It included tailored strategies for time management, stress alleviation, and goal setting. Anna's package wasn't just a service but a call to a transformative adventure.

Real-World Case Study:
The Transformational Wellness Journey

Sarah, a driven professional, was grappling with aligning her corporate ambitions with her well-being. Amanda's distinct coaching offer, which promised more than mere guidance, piqued her interest. This journey led Sarah to redefine her priorities, understand her core values, and carve out a wellness roadmap. What started as a mere offer transitioned into a transformative chapter for Sarah. This profound impact had her advocating Amanda's expertise, leading many of her peers to a similar transformation.

The Secret Sauce: Personalization and Tangible Outcomes

A resonating offer isn't just about promises; it's about manifesting tangible outcomes. The magic lies in tailoring the experience and sketching a clear path to success. The goal is to address the challenges and offer actionable blueprints that prompt immediate positive shifts.

A business coach, Jake infused his offers with more than just coaching. His packages embraced personalized growth blueprints, interactive workshops, and an accountability partner. This resonated with entrepreneurs looking to take their businesses to the next level.

Real-World Case Study: The Startup Scaling Odyssey

For Alex, an e-commerce entrepreneur, growth had become elusive. Jake's unique offer promised a bespoke roadmap to scaling success. This engagement led Alex to delve into optimizing business operations, identifying fresh markets, and bolstering customer retention tactics. The endgame? A thriving startup and a beeline of prospective investors.

The Nuances of Crafting Your Offer

While coaching holds universal principles, each coach brings a unique flavor. The road to crafting your distinct offer can be challenging. Here, the insights of an adept business coach can be a game-changer. They can offer tailored guidance, allowing you to narrow down, pinpoint your ideal clientele, and polish your unique selling proposition (USP) and intellectual property (IP). With their insights, you can sculpt an offer that resonates with your audience and mirrors your coaching values.

The case studies underscore a vital truth: Crafting compelling offers melds art with science. It demands a deep dive into the psyche of your audience, grasping their challenges, and presenting solutions that promise transformation. Your coaching offer isn't just a service; it's a commitment, a transformative journey, and an emblem of your dedication to your client's success.

Tip #1: Personal branding is crucial. With a saturated market, coaches who stand out online and offline with a unique value proposition almost always succeed.

Tip #2: Use the reverse-engineering method. Ask your existing clients what made them say yes to you. This feedback is gold in refining your offers.

Tip #3: Offer a Mystery Mentor session, where the client gets a surprise guest mentor for one session. This unexpected twist can create buzz and intrigue.

Secret #1: Use the Mystery Box tactic. Offer a valuable bonus whose details remain undisclosed until purchase. This curiosity can be a significant motivator.

Secret #2: Crafting a compelling offer goes beyond the tangible value. It's about the intangible transformation you offer your clients. Can you get them from point A to B in their lives? That journey and how you communicate it can be your unique selling point.

Gold Nugget: Emotion is the currency of conversion. While logic can initiate interest, the emotional connection of an offer triggers action. Ensure your offers tap into your potential clients' emotional needs and desires.

Fun Fact: Historical pillars—the stone kind—often had a slight swelling or entasis. This was an optical illusion trick; they appeared straight to the human eye despite their curvature. Similarly, your coaching pillars might need subtle tweaks to appear perfect.

Cheat Sheet for Irresistible Offers:

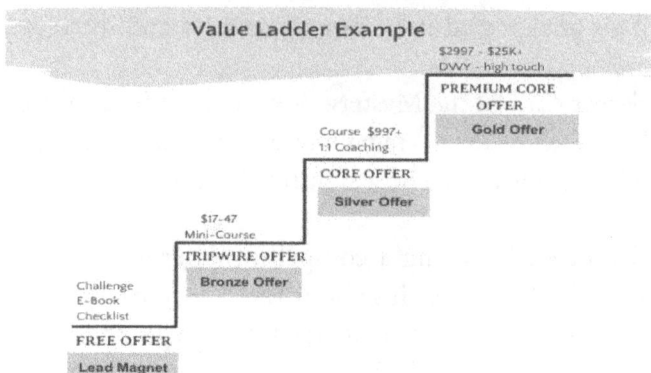

Value Ladder Example

For those seeking to master the art of a compelling offer, below is a consolidated guide.

GUIDE TO CREATING AN IRRESISTIBLE OFFER

1. Define your niche and ideal client.
2. Dive deep into competitor research.
3. Pinpoint your USP.
4. Distill your transformational journey into three to five steps (your IP).
5. Construct a comprehensive offer package that includes:

   1. The container
   2. Shortest path to desired results

3. Competitive pricing
4. FAQs addressing potential reservations
5. Introduce scarcity and urgency
6. Present a risk-reversal strategy
7. Enrich your IP with added value
8. Incorporate bonuses, perhaps one addressing post-transformation challenges (e.g., for weight loss, offer a style guide for the newly fit)
9. Design a persuasive sales page with lucid messaging
10. Employ a launch strategy
11. Validate and test your offer
12. Amplify organically across all of your social media channels
13. Mull over paid promotions
14. Monitor analytics and refine as needed
15. Always have exceptional customer support and fulfillment
16. Engage and nurture post-purchase
17. Ask for testimonials
18. Encourage and ask for referrals

Summary:

Dive into the art and science behind constructing offers that grab attention and lead to massive client conversions.

Your offer becomes appealing by weaving your clear and authentic messaging with your unique selling proposition and proprietary intellectual property. It emerges as a beacon in a crowded marketplace, calling to those who resonate with your vision.

If you'd like to create a value ladder of different tiered offers that creates consistent revenue in your business, join us in The Elite Entrepreneur. https://pursueand-thrive.com/elite-entrepreneur

Action Points:

1. Review your current offerings. Are they clear, compelling, and tailored to your target audience?
2. Draft a new offer based on the insights from this chapter.
3. A/B test your new offer with a small segment of your audience to gather feedback.

CHAPTER 3

Mastering the Message: The Voice that Resonates

In today's digital landscape flooded with fleeting attention spans and infinite choices, the strength and clarity of your message will be the pivotal factor that elevates you above the sea of cookie-cutter coaches. In this chapter, we uncover the nuances of messaging mastery—an essential skill in establishing an authentic connection with your audience and driving them to action.

The Essence of Authentic Messaging

Imagine your message as the heartbeat of your coaching brand—a rhythmic pulse that reflects your core values and speaks to your audience's innermost aspirations. Crafting an impactful message is not just about communication but connection. As my favorite mentor says, "The messaging is the most critical piece of your offer." Whether elucidating your coaching ethos, spotlighting your services, or unveiling transformative offers, your message's clarity and authenticity set the stage for deep engagement.

A potential client whose soul resonates with your message is a gateway to lasting commitment. So, how do you sculpt messages that genuinely mirror your coaching vision while striking a chord with your target audience?

Golden Guidelines for Authentic Messaging

1. **Lead with Empathy:** Every compelling message is anchored in empathy. Dive deep into understanding your audience's challenges, desires, and dreams. By resonating with their emotional landscape, you pave the way for messages that touch hearts and change minds.

2. **Simplicity is key:** In a world drowning in jargon and overcomplication, simplicity stands out. Aim for directness and clarity, ensuring even your most intricate ideas are accessible and relatable. I can't emphasize this enough! Even the CEO of a billion-dollar company doesn't want to waste brain cells reading jargon. It's not impressive; it actually hurts to read it.

3. **Fill it with Emotion:** Stirring emotions is the cornerstone of engagement. Design your

messages to evoke feelings that mirror your coaching expertise—be it empowerment, hope, or a burning desire for change. It's through emotions that your words transform into action.

4. **The Power and Magic is Storytelling:** Stories have always had this captivating charm for me, pulling folks into a world of change and wonder. I often think about the hurdles I've jumped, the changes I sparked, and the wins I sweat for. Sharing these tales feels like building bridges, connecting me closer to those I share them with. Here's a little secret I've learned along the way: People are drawn to connect with you—the individual behind the brand. When they hear your story, they're not just buying a program or service but investing in a bond with you. That genuine connection, that feeling of truly understanding and being understood, is the magic touch that turns potential clients into devoted followers.

5. **Brand Voice—My Secret Ingredient**: Beyond the fancy words and catchy phrases, I've always believed the unique tone and steady rhythm of our brand voice leaves a mark. It's like a signature melody playing gently in the background, guiding folks closer. Whether it's a dash of empowerment, a sprinkle of care, or a strong, authoritative note, it's this distinct flavor that folks come to recognize, trust, and

come back for. It's more than just a voice; it's our brand's unique heartbeat.

Digging Deeper: When Messaging Truly Shines

Envision your unique coaching program as a shining light waiting to change lives. The way you talk about it is the magnet pulling people in. With real, genuine words, your message doesn't just tell; it inspires, relates, and sparks action.

Think about Jane, an entrepreneur filled with drive but looking for guidance. When she stumbles upon your words, it's like they're crafted just for her. It's more than just information; it feels like a conversation, understanding her dreams and recognizing the hurdles she faces. That genuine connection is what nudges her to dive into your coaching world.

As you navigate the world of powerful communication, remember that authentic messages aren't just heard; they're felt. Recognize the magic of real, relatable messaging to truly make an impact. Dive deep, harness its potential, and witness your coaching business flourish like never before.

Tip: Share past wins and losses; share your journey— the good and the bad. Your flaws, failures, and hiccups aren't weaknesses; they're absolute content gold mines! Sharing vulnerabilities can build stronger connections more than any perfectly crafted message can. It's this human touch that truly connects.

Secret: Employ ambient soundscapes during your sessions (like forest sounds or cafe ambiance). This can subtly elevate mood and enhance concentration.

Gold Nugget #1: The daily hamster wheel of content creation can distract you from your core messaging. Avoid falling into the trap of creating content for content's sake. Only post when you feel it inside of you. This is your brand. If you're putting out crappy content because "Everyone else is posting daily," you're following the herd, and your brand will pay the price. Instead, ensure every piece aligns with your core messaging and adds genuine value.

Gold Nugget #2: Occasionally send hand-written letters or postcards to your clients. In a digital age, a personal touch stands out and creates deep emotional connections.

Fun Fact: In marketing lore, the original irresistible offer was a set of Ginsu Knives on TV in the 1970s. Not only could they cut through cans, but they also came with a fifty-year guarantee. There's still time to get our money back!

Summary: You learned the significance of crafting an authentic and impactful message in today's crowded digital landscape. This chapter underscores the pillars of genuine messaging—empathy, simplicity, emotion, storytelling, and brand voice—as tools to deeply connect with and inspire one's audience. Through authentic communication, coaches can elevate their brand, create meaningful relationships, and stand out in a saturated market.

If you want to uncover the power of clear, relatable messaging and how it can transform your connection with potential clients and effortlessly sell your offers, join us in The Elite Entrepreneur. https://pursueandthrive.com/elite-entrepreneur

Action Points:

1. Reevaluate your current messaging. Does it resonate with your target audience's needs and emotions?
2. Craft a new core message for your coaching business.
3. Test the new messaging on your website and social media and observe the engagement.

In the following chapter, we'll investigate the twin pillars of credibility and authority. Understanding and cultivating these qualities are paramount for any coach wishing to leave an indelible mark on the industry.

CHAPTER 4

Establishing Credibility and Authority

Coaching is as much about expertise as it is about trust. While a rich foundation of knowledge is essential, the perceived value of that knowledge hinges largely on the credibility and authority you possess in your niche. This chapter dives into the nuanced world of gaining and maintaining a reputation that compels clients to believe in you, trust your guidance, and act on your advice.

The Dual Pillars: Credibility and Authority

Credibility stems from being trustworthy and reliable, while authority is rooted in acknowledged expertise and leadership in a field. Together, they form a potent mix that convinces clients of your capability. However, establishing them isn't an event; it's a process, built over time, client by client, success by success.

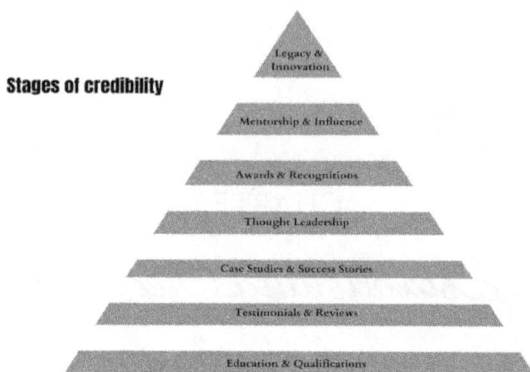

Stages of credibility

Pyramid from bottom to top:
- Education & Qualifications
- Testimonials & Reviews
- Case Studies & Success Stories
- Thought Leadership
- Awards & Recognitions
- Mentorship & Influence
- Legacy & Innovation

Strategies to Fortify Your Position

1. **Showcase Your Journey:** Authenticity always wins. Share your journey. It may not be pretty. It most likely is a little messy, and honestly, your following is most likely on a rollercoaster journey, too. Get vulnerable and real about how you arrived at this point, the challenges you faced, and the wisdom you acquired. Clients always resonate more with real stories than with your credentials.

2. **Leverage Testimonials:** Nothing speaks louder than the words of satisfied clients. Encourage testimonials and showcase them prominently. They serve as evidence of your effectiveness. Regularly send out emails to those you have worked with or purchased your digital courses, etc., and ask them to give a testimonial. For those you have worked

with one-on-one, get full case studies. For those who may not know you personally, ask them to give you a shout-out on social media about what they've learned and love about your course.

3. **Engage in Continuous Learning:** The coaching world has exploded, and if you're not keeping up to date with what's happening, you'll fall behind—fast! Regularly update your knowledge, get certifications if necessary, and make it known that you're always advancing. It shows your commitment and expertise.

4. **Host Workshops and Webinars:** Active engagement with your audience provides value and positions you as an expert. Workshops and webinars can help your following with their common problems. Additionally, these sessions allow you to offer solutions and a taste of your coaching style.

5. **Publish Content:** Whether through a blog, podcast, or YouTube channel, regularly delivering value-packed content cements your authority over time. It showcases your depth of knowledge and keeps you visible. Again, be authentic. If you make a mistake, big deal, keep going. Share the struggles you have faced along with the wins. The coach who only talks about her wins dancing around in every story and reel has put up a front.

Credibility Booster: A Fast-Track to Enhancing Credibility

One of the quickest ways to enhance your credibility is through targeted interventions like Credibility Booster, created by Mitchell Levy, a global credibility expert. This four-hour intensive program provides the clarity you need to highlight and bolster your credibility. From fine-tuning how you appear on platforms like LinkedIn to succinctly articulating your value proposition, Credibility Boosters offer actionable steps to show that you are credible and stand out in your marketplace.

To know more about Credibility Booster and its potential to transform your credibility profile, connect at ask@pursueandthrive.com, and we will set you up for the next available Credibility Booster.

The Ripple Effect of Credibility and Authority

Imagine you've assisted a client named Michael with achieving a significant professional breakthrough. Michael's success story, when shared, acts as a ripple, influencing potential clients who hear about it. Such tangible results, combined with strategic efforts to bolster your credibility and authority, solidify your reputation.

Your influence extends far beyond a single coaching session. It's a blend of the trust you nurture, the expertise you exhibit, and the results you consistently deliver.

Tip: Collaborate with influencers from different niches. A joint webinar or workshop with someone who doesn't offer coaching will offer fresh perspectives and expose you to an audience you'd typically never reach.

Secret: Establishing authority isn't just about showcasing your credentials but demonstrating your commitment to ongoing learning and adaptation. Attend industry conferences, participate in webinars, and constantly update your skill set. Your audience will notice.

Gold Nugget #1: Authentic testimonials and reviews can skyrocket your credibility. Strongly encourage your happy clients to share their experience working with you and the results from your course or program. Sprinkle these all over. Add them to your website, emails, sales pages, and signature block, and post them on all your social media platforms, etc. Tag the person who gave you the testimonial so they can see how much you appreciate them. Ask them to give you a shout-out and tag you.

Gold Nugget #2: Podcast guesting is an often overlooked but powerful strategy. You can talk to thousands (sometimes tens of thousands) of your ideal clients on any given day—for free. It establishes authority, reaches new audiences, and builds backlinks to boost your online presence.

Gold Nugget #3: Occasionally chat about a book or movie you've recently read or watched. Relate its themes to real-life or business experiences. It's a great way to show your following that you're not all business, and you get the bigger picture.

Fun Fact: The term branding originated from the age-old practice of livestock branding, where ranchers marked their cattle with a unique symbol. Just as they made their herd distinguishable, your brand should stand out in the coaching crowd.

As we conclude this chapter, remember: The journey to establishing credibility and authority will always be ongoing. With every client success story, insightful content piece, and genuine engagement, you create your legacy of trust and expertise. In our next chapter, we will dive into scaling strategies, ensuring that as your reputation grows, your coaching business does, too.

Summary:

Understand the pivotal role of trust in coaching and learn methods to strengthen your standing as a trusted expert.

If you'd like clarity and a credible coaching brand, join us in The Elite Entrepreneur. https://pursueandthrive. com/elite-entrepreneur

Action Points:

1. Identify three actions you can take this month to boost your credibility. (Hint: Sign up for a Credibility Booster.)
2. Seek testimonials from past clients and sprinkle them everywhere.
3. Consider writing guest articles or appearing on podcasts to further establish authority.

CHAPTER 5

Scaling Beyond Startup: Strategies for Sustainable Growth

B uilding a coaching venture is much like construct-ing a skyscraper. You start with a foundational idea, sturdy and grounded. Then, brick by brick, strategy by strategy, you keep adding floors, reaching for the sky.

The Evolution from Startup to Scalability

You began with a plot of land (your unique coaching idea) and laid a strong foundation (your startup phase). As you add more floors (clients and strategies), your structure's impact and visibility grow. The question is, how do you ensure this architectural marvel doesn't wobble?

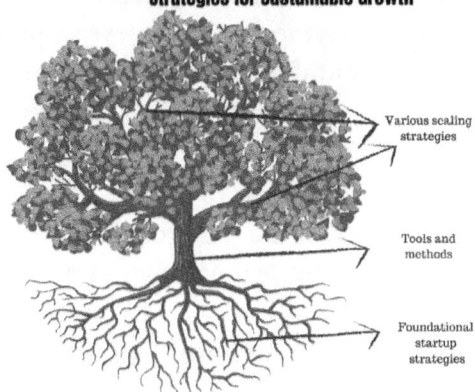

Strategies for Sustainable Growth

Various scaling strategies

Tools and methods

Foundational startup strategies

Advanced Strategies for Sustainable Growth

1. **Signature Systems and Frameworks:** Think of these as the architectural blueprints for your skyscraper. Your unique methodologies provide clarity and guidance, ensuring every new floor aligns perfectly.

2. **Group Coaching and Masterminds:** This is the elevator in your building, allowing you to reach more people faster. The communal vibe? That's the coffee shop on the ground floor, where clients gather, share, and inspire.

3. **Premium Offerings and Upsells:** These are the penthouse suites. As your reputation grows, offer premium spaces for those wanting more luxury (or in-depth guidance).

4. **Automation and Systems Integration:** Imagine trying to water every plant in a massive building manually. Not fun, right? Automation is your built-in sprinkler system, ensuring things run smoothly.

5. **Thought Leadership and Content Strategy:** This is the neon sign on your skyscraper's roof, ensuring people miles away know who you are and what you stand for.

6. **Advanced Accountability and Measurement:** Of course, there are regular building inspections. Use data-driven strategies to ensure your structure remains sound as it grows.

Real-World Application: Elevating Growth Through Advanced Strategies

Picture Sarah, another coach turned architect. As her coaching skyscraper grew, she introduced group sessions and premium offerings. What about her content—that neon sign we talked about? As she integrated automation, her plants never went thirsty.

Embracing Sustainable Growth

Your coaching skyscraper isn't just any building; it's a beacon of transformation and growth. With these advanced strategies, it will stand tall and shine brilliantly in the city skyline of the coaching world.

Tip #1: Employ VR or AR technology. Imagine a coaching session where clients wear VR headsets and are transported to a serene beach or calm forest. It's an experience they won't forget.

Tip #2: Creating multiple income streams can be a game-changer. Add in low-, mid-, and high-ticket digital products, courses, and/or group coaching sessions and VIP retreat experiences.

Tip #3: Create a referral program. Encourage your satisfied clients to refer you to their network in exchange for a free program or service, or create an affiliate program where they receive a certain percentage for each client they refer. I suggest a 30 to 50 percent affiliate payout. Organic, word-of-mouth referrals can sometimes be more effective than paid marketing.

Secret #1: Host a Failure Forum. Instead of only celebrating successes, occasionally discuss what didn't work and why. This level of authenticity and openness can resonate deeply with an audience tired of perennial success stories.

Secret #2: In the age of relentless emails, social media notifications, and DMs, remember: Your time and energy are precious. Instead of trying to do *everything*, prioritize tasks that directly lead to monetization. For instance, instead of spending hours crafting the perfect Instagram post, focus on creating a solid sales funnel or refining your coaching program.

Gold Nugget: As you scale, understand the importance of delegation. You must hand off tasks that aren't bringing in money. Even if you think you're not ready, trust me: Hire before you feel ready. If you wait until you're swamped, you won't have the time or patience to find the right fit and train them properly. Keep your eyes on what fuels your coaching growth, and let someone else handle the rest.

Fun Fact: The word strategy is derived from the Greek word strategos, meaning the art of the general. So, just like a general, you're preparing for success on the business battlefield.

Summary:

We talked about navigating the journey from startup to scale gaining insights into advanced growth strategies for your coaching venture.

To get your personalized, step-by-step process from startup to scaling for your coaching business, join us in The Elite Entrepreneur. https://pursueandthrive.com/elite-entrepreneur

Action Points:

1. Assess your current business size and determine the next growth stage.

2. Implement at least one scaling strategy from this chapter.

3. Regularly review and adjust your strategy based on feedback and results.

CHAPTER 6

Overcoming Growth Pains: Solutions for Progress

Scaling is exhilarating. It's like riding a roller coaster with its thrilling highs. However, just like a roller coaster, there are unexpected drops.

The Struggle of Doing All the Things

As a coach, sometimes it feels like you're trying to juggle while riding a unicycle on that roller coaster. It's tempting to be the jack-of-all-trades, but master-of-none syndrome will quickly send your cart off the rails.

Breaking Free from Shiny Object Syndrome

Oh, look, another flashy roller coaster! It promises a smoother ride and bigger thrills. Constantly switching rides is a one-way ticket to Dizzyville and wasted days, weeks, months, and, sometimes, years.

The Pitfalls of Non-Revenue-Generating Tasks

These tasks are the roller coaster's photo booth. Sure, you get a fun memory, but it won't move your coaching journey forward.

Strategies for Progress: A Guide to Thriving

1. **Delegation and Outsourcing:** I get it. Handing over the reins can be tough, but trust me, you can't be everywhere at once. When I finally let go and brought in some pros to handle tasks outside my wheelhouse, things ran more smoothly, and I had more time to focus on what I truly loved doing.

2. **Focused Decision-Making:** Not every opportunity that comes knocking is the right fit. This is a lesson I learned along the way. Stick to choices that align with your vision. You don't have to chase every shiny thing.

3. **Time Blocking and Prioritization:** If there's one hack I swear by, it's setting dedicated time for tasks. No more juggling or multitasking. Allocate time slots, focus on the task at hand, and you'll see a change.

4. **Streamlined Systems and Automation:** Embracing the right tools was a game-changer for me. It's like having an extra pair of hands.

With the right systems, things flow, saving you time and headaches.

5. **Leveraging High-Level Coaching:** There's always something new to learn. Even though I've come a long way, I still lean on mentors. They've walked the path and seen the hurdles; their insights are pure gold.

Real-World Application: Implementing these strategies changed the game for folks I've known, like Sarah, and me. Mix them into your routine and watch your game elevate. I did, and it made all the difference.

Overcoming Growth Pains: Solutions for Progress

Progress in the Face of Challenges

Growth pains are a given on this thrilling ride of coaching. However, with your safety harness (strategies) secured, you're set for an exhilarating journey.

Tip: Try the Mentor Swap. Pair up with a coach from another industry and become each other's client for a month. This fresh perspective can unearth hidden pain points and opportunities.

Secret #1: Growth pains are often a sign of outdated processes. Embrace technology and automation to streamline your operations. Growth pains also indicate that you're on the verge of a breakthrough. Instead of retreating, lean into the pain, understand its origin, and innovate.

Secret #2: The most profound coaching breakthroughs sometimes come from places like art, music, and even culinary experiences. Diversifying your experiences can lead to more enriched coaching sessions.

Secret #3: Every top coach has had moments of doubt. It's not the absence of doubt but the courage to push past it that defines success.

Gold Nugget: Growth requires internal and external nurturing. While you're focused on growing the business, also invest in personal growth. Whether it's mental well-being, skill acquisition, or ensuring work-life balance, your evolution will influence your business success.

Fun Fact: Crystal balls, often associated with clairvoyance, have been used for scrying (seeing the future) since ancient times. But remember, in the coaching world, it's less about predicting the exact future and more about adapting to its changes.

Summary:

Unravel the common challenges faced during growth and arm yourself with solutions to keep progressing.

Learn to grow and scale easily with your personalized quarterly strategic blueprint in The Elite Entrepreneur program. https://pursueandthrive.com/elite-entrepreneur

Action Points:

1. List any current challenges or obstacles you're facing.
2. Apply at least one solution discussed in this chapter to address a current challenge.
3. Consider seeking mentorship or peer feedback when faced with unfamiliar challenges.

CHAPTER 7

Empowerment and Impact

Let's dive deep, folks. When I started my coaching journey, I never envisioned the profound transition from a budding entrepreneur to someone who could genuinely spark change in others. This chapter is about that evolution and the indelible mark you can leave.

From Start-Up Enthusiast to Change Catalyst

Coaching isn't just another feather in your entrepreneurial cap. It's creating moments when you see someone's inner light bulb turn on and realize they can climb mountains they once thought insurmountable. As someone who's been on both sides of the table, I can't emphasize enough that your influence isn't just about the lessons you teach; it's about the mindset shifts you facilitate.

Here's a nugget from my playbook: Mastery doesn't arrive overnight. I, too, leaned heavily on many coaches and mentors, soaking up their wisdom to shape my coaching path.

Every impactful coach I've met, myself included, can pinpoint mentors who elevated their game. A coach without guidance is like a tree without roots. Mentorship equips you with fresh perspectives and novel strategies and reignites passion when you need a boost.

If there's a secret sauce to my coaching journey, it's a commitment to constant learning. I embrace every workshop, every piece of feedback, and every new strategy and mold it into something that serves my unique coaching style.

Pillars of an Impactful Coach

1. **Unwavering Drive:** You must have grit. You must have resilience. Unwavering drive is about staying the course, riding out the challenges, and constantly searching for those little golden tidbits that elevate your coaching style. There will be tears and jumping-for-joy moments that make up for the tears.

2. **Evergreen Learning:** The learning curve never ends, and that's the beauty of it. When I started coaching, I gave up watching TV, put my nose to the grindstone, and never looked

back. Dive into books, listen to podcasts, attend seminars, and never stop absorbing.

3. **Genuine Connection:** One thing I've prided myself on is connecting. That soul-to-soul bond with your clients paves the way for authentic transformation. I have at least five Zoom coffee chats a week. I love meeting new people and seeing how I can help or who I can connect them with.

4. **Strategic Vision:** It's not just about tackling what's right in front of you. It's the art of peeling back layers, understanding the broader journey, and plotting a course for the long haul. Start with the end in mind.

Your Ripple in the Pond

When the curtains close on a coaching session, the real magic begins. That feeling when a client tells you how they conquered a fear of going live or had a massive launch because of a strategy you co-created is priceless. That, my friend, is the echo of your influence—a legacy that lives on, touching lives in ways you might not even realize.

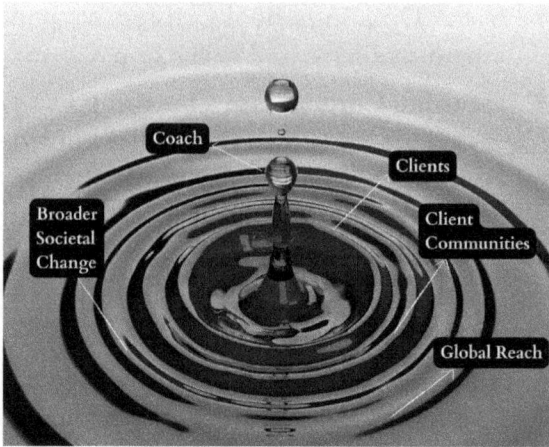

Tip #1: Organize silent retreats for your clients where the focus is on introspection and self-awareness rather than external input. The insights derived from silence can often be profound.

Tip #2: Document your journey and encourage your clients to do the same. These journey logs become invaluable testimonials, case studies, and content assets.

Gold Nugget: Organize a "Flashback Day" for clients, taking them through a journey of art, culture, and knowledge from a particular historical era. Link lessons from that era to modern-day challenges.

Fun Fact: Coaching isn't just a Western concept. Traditional forms of coaching and mentoring can be traced back to ancient civilizations, from the philosophical teachings in Greece to the guru-shishya tradition in India.

Summary:

Reflect on the broader vision of your coaching journey and the impact you wish to make.

Join us in The Elite Entrepreneur, where you will learn what is needed to be an empowered and impactful coach. https://pursueandthrive.com/elite-entrepreneur

Remember that your coaching journey is like the evolution from spark to torchbearer. It's a constant cycle of lighting, guiding, and growing. Keep your flame alive, seek new firewood, and continue to light the path for others.

Action Points:

1. Write your vision statement if you haven't already.
2. Identify three steps to align your current efforts more closely with your vision.
3. Share your vision with your community to inspire and attract like-minded individuals.

CHAPTER 8

Authenticity Over Amplification: The Genuine Coach's Guide to Standing Out

In the ever-growing world of coaching, it's become all too common to hear voices that seem to say, "Look at me! Buy my course! Read my book!" While self-promotion is essential in any business, there's a delicate balance to maintain. The best coaches understand one fundamental truth: Clients are less interested in *you* and more interested in *how you can help them*.

1. The Me-Centric Approach: A Common Pitfall

Today, many coaches fall into the trap of a me-centric approach. Their content revolves around their achievements, their offerings, and their journey. While sharing your story is essential for building credibility, it's crucial to ask: "Am I making this all about me, or am I genuinely focusing on the needs of my potential clients?"

2. **Your Clients' Real Needs: Beyond Courses and Books**

Let's clarify something essential: Your clients aren't just looking to purchase a course, book, or webinar. In truth, they're seeking solutions to their challenges, answers to their burning questions, and guidance on their personal or professional journeys. They are more inclined to invest in a coach with whom they deeply resonate. Your story, experiences, and unique journey matter immensely. While your program or book might be the tool, they're genuinely investing in the transformation and results they believe you can usher them into with your unique narrative.

3. **Confidence Without Ego**

It's essential to project confidence in your expertise. Clients want to trust that you know your stuff. However, there's a difference between showcasing your knowledge and drowning in overconfidence. Genuine confidence is appealing; an overinflated ego is a deterrent. The best coaches exude a quiet confidence that says, "I've got you," without overshadowing the client's needs.

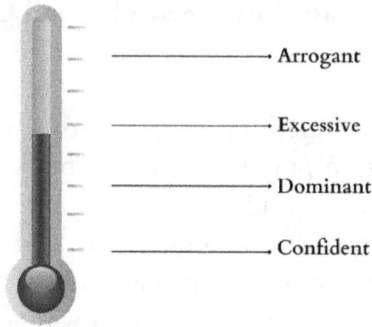

Arrogant

Excessive

Dominant

Confident

4. From "Look At Me" to "I See You"

Transition from a "look at me" mindset to an "I see you" approach. Recognize the struggles, aspirations, and dreams of your clients. They're more likely to trust in your guidance when they feel seen and understood. It's about creating content and courses that resonate with their needs rather than merely promoting what you've created.

5. Building Authentic, Client-Centric Connections

In the heart of coaching lies the art of connection. The most influential coaches are those who build authentic, client-focused relationships. When clients feel you're genuinely invested in their growth and not just selling a product, they're more likely to engage, refer, and return.

Tip #1: Develop an "Echo Feedback" system. Instead of just taking feedback, echo what you understood to the client. This reflective method can sometimes unearth deeper insights.

Tip #2: Set unplugged days. These are days when you disconnect from all digital platforms and just reflect, ideate, and rejuvenate. In a hyper-connected world, occasional disconnection can lead to clearer thinking and better strategies.

Secret #1: Create a digital avatar or an alter ego for your coaching brand. This persona can offer advice, tips, and tricks in a playful, unique manner, setting you apart in a saturated market.

Secret #2: The journey to coaching excellence is a marathon, not a sprint. It's about consistent, small actions every day. Remember, the best coaches are eternal students, always seeking to learn, evolve, and adapt.

Gold Nugget #1: Consider reverse testimonials. Instead of just clients praising you, offer testimonials where you praise your clients and their journeys. Give shout-outs in posts and emails and tag them on social media. This mutual respect and acknowledgment can humanize your brand and resonate with future clients.

Gold Nugget #2: Authenticity is felt, not told. It's in the way you interact with clients, the stories you tell, and the values you uphold. In a world that often prioritizes amplification, staying genuine will make you stand out, unlike those who coach merely for the spotlight.

Gold Nugget #3: The best coaches often aren't those with the most qualifications but those with the most empathy and intuition. Your instincts can be as powerful, if not more so, than learned techniques.

Fun Fact #1: The concept of adding value can be seen in nature. For instance, honey bees transform simple nectar into honey, adding value to what they collect and making it last longer and taste sweeter.

Fun Fact #2: The word authentic comes from the Greek word athentikos, which means original. Essentially, being authentic is all about being an original in a world full of copycats.

Summary:

Embrace authenticity in your coaching practice, understanding its power in distinguishing you in a saturated market. Your role as a coach extends beyond courses, books, or webinars. It's about understanding, connecting, and genuinely aiding in the transformation of your clients. In the loud marketplace of coaching, the voices that resonate most deeply aren't the loudest voices in the room or the ones constantly talking about themselves but those genuinely focused on the growth and success of others. Be that voice. Remember, clients don't just invest in a coach; they invest in a genuine partner for their journey.

Join us in The Elite Entrepreneur, where you will be coached by an authentic and genuine coach and learn to embrace this for your business, which will ensure your success. https://pursueandthrive.com/elite-entrepreneur

Action Points:

1. Reflect on any areas where you might be compromising your authenticity.
2. Implement strategies from this chapter to enhance genuine connections with clients.
3. Share personal stories or experiences on your platforms to further humanize and authenticate your brand.

Conclusion

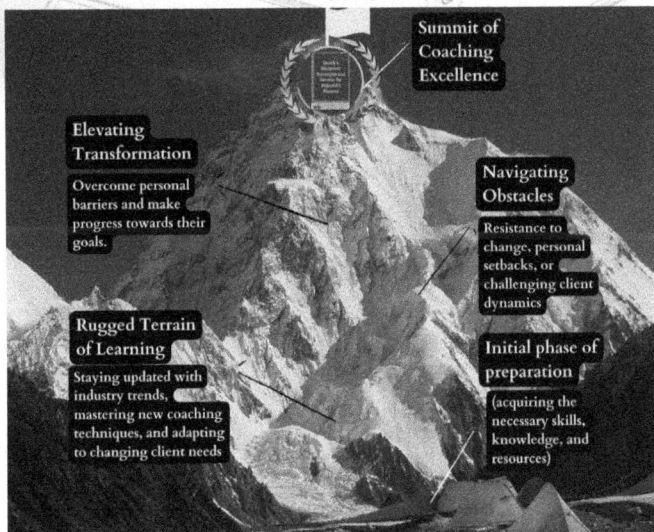

Summit of Coaching Excellence

Elevating Transformation
Overcome personal barriers and make progress towards their goals.

Navigating Obstacles
Resistance to change, personal setbacks, or challenging client dynamics

Rugged Terrain of Learning
Staying updated with industry trends, mastering new coaching techniques, and adapting to changing client needs

Initial phase of preparation
(acquiring the necessary skills, knowledge, and resources)

As we wind down our time in this book, imagine us in a relaxed setting, reflecting on everything we've covered and eagerly looking ahead. (Note how I'm using visualization here—wink, wink—which this book mentions as a must-do technique for writing your company's copy, including your emails, sales pages, etc.) Coaching isn't about solitary growth; it's about mutual learning, building connections, and evolving together.

Let's recap all of the juicy details from Chapters 1 to 8:

1. **Always Learning, Always Leading**: Behind every successful coach is a guiding mentor. Striving for mastery means being both the teacher and the student.

2. **Speak Your Truth:** Authenticity is the cornerstone of real connections. Speak from the heart, and your message will resonate.

3. **Turning Visions into Realities**: Coaching transcends mere transactions; it's about making dreams tangible.

4. **Mapping Out Success:** In the dynamic world of coaching, having a clear plan transforms every hurdle into a growth opportunity.

5. **The Trust Factor:** Trust isn't just about building a brand; it's about cultivating genuine relationships.

6. **Beyond the Coach Title:** Your role transcends its title, acting as a guiding beacon for your clients when they seek direction.

7. **Lighting the Path:** Transition from an entrepreneur to a torchbearer, becoming an empowering beacon for others to follow.

8. **Authenticity Over Amplification:** Transition from self-centered promotion to genuine connection, prioritizing your client's growth and success in a saturated coaching market.

If you want these essential foundations of coaching in your business, join us in The Elite Entrepreneur. https://pursueandthrive.com/elite-entrepreneur

Fun Fact: The word conclusion stems from the Latin *concludere*, meaning to shut up or confine. However, in the coaching world, a conclusion isn't an end; it's a new beginning, a launchpad to greater success.

Appendix

COMPREHENSIVE GLOSSARY FOR COACHING AND BUSINESS

This all-encompassing glossary offers a clear understanding of pivotal terms you most likely will come across in the coaching business sphere, depending on your niche.

360-Degree Feedback: A process where employees receive confidential, anonymous feedback from those around them, often used in executive coaching.

Action Plan: A detailed sequence of steps or activities to achieve specific goals.

Benchmarking: Comparing one's business processes and metrics to industry bests or best practices.

Boundary Setting: Creating clear limits to maintain a healthy work-life balance and mental well-being.

Branding: Creating a unique name and image for a product or business in consumers' minds.

Breakthrough: A significant or sudden advance, discovery, or development in the coaching process.

Business Model Canvas: A strategic management template for developing new or documenting existing business models.

Cash Flow Management: The tracking of money entering and leaving a business.

Certified Coach: An individual who has completed the required training and examinations from a recognized coaching institution.

Client-Centered: A coaching approach where the client's strengths, needs, and values are central to the coaching process.

Discovery Session: An introductory session where the coach and client explore goals, challenges, and the potential coaching journey.

Elevator Pitch: A concise, persuasive speech used to spark interest in what an individual or organization does.

Executive Presence: The ability to project gravitas, confidence, poise under pressure, and decisiveness.

Feedback Loop: A mechanism where the coach provides constructive feedback, and the client responds, ensuring effective communication and progress.

Goals vs. Outcomes: While goals are specific objectives one intends to achieve, outcomes are the broader impacts or results of achieving those goals.

GROW Model: A structured method for problem-solving and goal setting, standing for Goal, Reality, Options, and Way forward.

Holistic Coaching: An approach that considers the client's physical, mental, and emotional well-being.

IP (Intellectual Property): Refers to creations of the mind, like inventions and literary works. Protected by law, allowing creators to earn from their inventions.

Key Performance Indicator (KPI): A measurable value indicating how effectively a company achieves key business objectives.

Leadership Pipeline: A structured process showing how leadership requirements increase at each subsequent level.

Mentorship Program: A professional relationship where a more experienced person guides a less experienced individual.

Mindset Shift: A fundamental change in an individual's attitudes or beliefs.

Niche Coaching: Specialized coaching that focuses on a specific sector or category of clients.

Ontological Coaching: A type of coaching focused on the being aspect of a person, exploring their way of being in the world.

Operational Efficiency: Delivering products or services most cost-effectively without sacrificing quality.

Paradigm Shift: A fundamental change in approach or underlying beliefs.

PESTLE Analysis: A tool used to scan an organization's external macro-environment, encompassing Political, Economic, Social, Technological, Legal, and Environmental factors.

Reflective Listening: A communication strategy where the coach listens and then mirrors what they've heard to the client.

Return on Investment (ROI): A performance measure evaluating the profitability of an investment.

Scale (Scaling): The capacity of a business to grow without compromising performance or efficiency.

Stakeholder Management: Systematic actions designed to engage with stakeholders.

SWOT Analysis: A tool used for strategic planning, identifying Strengths, Weaknesses, Opportunities, and Threats.

Talent Management: The anticipation and planning of human capital needs for an organization.

USP (Unique Selling Proposition): The unique benefit of a product, service, or brand distinguishing it in the marketplace.

Value Proposition: A statement explaining how a product or service solves a customer's problems or improves their situation.

Values Assessment: A tool or process to identify an individual's core beliefs and motivations.

Visioning: A process determining and articulating long-term business goals.

Visualization: A technique used to create a mental image of a future event, aiding in goal achievement.

Work-Life Integration: Blending personal and professional lives without fully merging them.

FAQ's: DEMYSTIFYING COACHING

This FAQ section addresses various concerns and misconceptions about coaching I've been confronted with over the years. These answers will help you help others around you better understand the coaching process and all its benefits.

1. What exactly is coaching?

Coaching is a partnership between the coach and the client, where the coach supports the client in achieving personal or professional goals through the process of self-discovery, strategizing, and accountability.

2. How is coaching different from therapy or counseling?

While both are valuable, they serve different purposes. Therapy often deals with healing past traumas and psychological issues, while coaching is forward focused, aiming to help clients set and achieve goals, make decisions, or develop skills.

3. Do I need a certified coach?

A certified coach has undergone specific training and met standards set by coaching institutions. While certification indicates a coach's dedication to their craft, it's essential to choose a coach you resonate with, whether certified or not. So, the short answer is no.

Look for a coach who has your values and lives the way you want to live.

4. How long does a typical coaching relationship last?

The duration varies. Some clients might achieve their goals in a few sessions, while others benefit from longer engagements. It's about what works best for the individual. I have a client who signed on in 2018, and we still meet.

5. Is coaching confidential?

Absolutely! Trust is a cornerstone of the coaching relationship. A professional coach upholds strict confidentiality standards, barring any legal reasons to share information.

6. Do I need to meet my coach in person?

While face-to-face sessions can be beneficial, many coaches work with clients over the phone, video calls (Zoom), or even email. It's about what's most convenient and comfortable for both parties.

7. What's the difference between coaching and mentoring?

While both support growth, mentoring usually involves someone experienced in a field guiding someone less experienced by sharing knowledge and insights. Conversely, coaching often involves empowering clients to discover their answers through guided questioning and exploration.

8. Is coaching just another trend?

Coaching, in various forms, has been around for centuries. Its principles are based on well-established techniques and philosophies. The recent surge in its popularity speaks to its effectiveness, not its novelty.

9. What if I don't see results right away?

Personal development and change often take time. While some clients might experience aha moments early on, others may find that progress is gradual. Consistency and commitment are key.

10. Why do coaches charge the rates they do?

Coaching is an investment in personal or professional development. The rates reflect the coach's training, expertise, and the value they provide in facilitating transformative changes in their clients' lives.

11. Can't I just coach myself?

While self-reflection and self-help tools are valuable, a coach offers an objective perspective, dedicated support, and proven strategies tailored to individual needs—elements challenging to replicate entirely on one's own.

12. **What if I'm unsure about the direction I want to take in my life or career? Can coaching still help?**

Absolutely. Many people approach coaching precisely because they are seeking clarity. A coach can guide you through processes that help uncover passions, strengths, and paths you might not have considered.

CLIENT RELATIONSHIP MANAGEMENT IN COACHING

Client relationship management in coaching refers to the strategies, techniques, and systems coaches use to manage and analyze client interactions and data throughout the client's journey to improve the coach-client relationship, increase client retention, and drive client success.

Initial Connection

Discovery Sessions: Before starting the coaching journey, offering discovery or intake sessions is crucial. This helps in gauging client-coach compatibility and setting clear expectations. For high-ticket clients, sending a physical welcome package in the mail is nice. This can include a notepad, pen, journal, mug, beautiful workbook, etc., for the program they just signed up for.

Goal Setting: Clearly define and understand the client's objectives. What do they hope to achieve from coaching? *Always* start with the end in mind. I was certified in goal setting in 2021 through Michael Hyatt's Full Focus Planner Certified Pro program, which I highly recommend. One of the key takeaways is to set five-year, one-year, quarterly, monthly, weekly, and daily goals. Your three daily goals should lead you into the weekly goals, the weekly into the monthly, and so on.

Building Trust and Rapport

Active Listening: I talk about this a lot. Listening is a foundational skill in coaching. It's essential not just to hear the words but also to understand their emotions and motivations. I'm fortunate in that I feel I can read people's emotions and body language.

Confidentiality: Ensure your clients and team members know their information and discussions will always be confidential. This creates a safe space for open conversation.

Empathy: It's hard, actually darn near impossible, to be a good coach if you're not empathetic, even in business coaching. Connect with clients on an emotional level, showing genuine understanding and concern for their feelings and challenges.

Maintaining the Relationship

Regular Check-ins: If you are meeting one-on-one with clients, don't wait for scheduled sessions. Sending an occasional message or email can show clients you care about their progress and well-being.

Feedback: Regularly seek feedback by asking or sending surveys about your coaching process and programs. This can lead to adjustments that might better serve not only their needs but also the needs of future clients.

Boundaries: While being accessible is essential, set clear boundaries to maintain a professional relationship. This includes boundaries around communication times, payment terms, etc. I take pride in giving my clients extra time if needed, but it can be a slippery slope. If I have the extra fifteen minutes they need, I make it known that I can give them a few more minutes to make sure they're on the right path. If I don't have it, I say so, and if it's critical, we'll set up a quick call, or I'll open Voxer. I want to make sure they get the service they need. There may be weeks that our calls are cut shorter because a full hour isn't needed. You should also adhere to the deadlines you set with your pricing. If your special offer ends tonight at midnight, that's when it ends—no exceptions. People will learn this and make sure they hop in on time next time.

Managing Challenges

Conflict Resolution: If disagreements arise, address them directly and professionally. Far too often, things get pushed to the wayside, and the issue festers, leading to resentment and/or blowing your lid. Use active listening and avoid being defensive.

Reassessing Goals: Over time, a client's goals might change. Periodically reassess, perhaps when doing a quarterly SWOT, and adjust as necessary to keep the coaching relationship relevant and valuable.

Graceful Conclusions

Ending the relationship: Not all coaching relationships last forever. Whether due to achieved goals or other reasons, ensure the relationship's conclusion is positive and graceful.

Testimonials and Referrals: Clients who have a positive experience will be willing to provide a testimonial or refer others. But it's essential to ask gracefully and without pressure. I've had coaches ask me for a testimonial the first week in the relationship. To me, that is a red flag that things might only go downhill from there.

Aftercare

Follow-up: Even after formal coaching ends, check in occasionally to see how they're doing and if they've maintained or built on their achievements.

Resource Sharing: Share articles, books, or other resources that might be relevant to the client's continued growth.

Alumni Groups: Consider creating groups or communities for past clients to interact with, share their successes, and continue learning. The idea is to always have your clients coming back for more.

Tools and Systems

CRM Systems: Using dedicated CRM software can help manage client data, schedule sessions, and track progress. There are a lot of all-in-one platforms out there. For example, I use FG Funnels, which has CRM, invoicing, a calendar scheduler, a social media connection, a website, funnels, an email service, and much more. When I started in 2018, at one point, I had seven different platforms I was dealing with.

Communication Platforms: There are many ways to keep the lines of communication open; I prefer Slack, Zoom, and Voxer. Emails tend to get lost.

In essence, client relationship management in coaching revolves around the idea of putting the client first, understanding their needs, and continually striving to offer the best possible service. It's about building and maintaining a bond of trust and ensuring the coaching experience is fruitful and fulfilling for the client.

SELF-CARE AND BURNOUT PREVENTION TIPS FOR COACHES

1. Set Clear Boundaries

- Determine specific working hours and stick to them.
- Clearly communicate your availability to clients.
- Ensure you have regular breaks throughout the day and take time off when needed.

2. Prioritize Physical Health

- Engage in regular physical activity, whether a daily walk, yoga, or a more intense workout.
- Ensure a balanced diet and stay hydrated.
- Prioritize sleep; adequate rest is essential for mental clarity and energy.

3. Engage in Regular Self-Reflection

- Take time to reflect on your feelings and thoughts regularly.
- Journaling can be an effective way to process emotions and gain clarity.

4. Practice Mindfulness and Meditation

- Even a few minutes of meditation can reduce stress.

- Breathing exercises can be beneficial, especially between sessions or when feeling overwhelmed.

5. **Seek Supervision or Peer Support**

   - Just as therapy is recommended for therapists, coaching supervision can benefit coaches.
   - Peer support groups can offer a space to discuss challenges and share solutions.

6. **Schedule Personal Time**

   - Ensure you have time for activities you love, whether reading, gardening, painting, or any other hobby.
   - Spend quality time with loved ones.

7. **Limit Exposure to Secondary Trauma**

   - Depending on your coaching niche, this struggle is real. Be aware of the emotional toll of listening to clients' trauma stories.
   - If needed, seek support or therapy to process these emotions.

8. **Learn to Say "No"**

   - It's crucial to recognize when you have reached capacity and not to overburden yourself with too many clients or commitments.

For the love of all things, please learn to say no to save your sanity.

9. **Regularly Update Skills and Techniques**

- Attend workshops or courses on self-care and burnout prevention. Reach out if you'd like the names of coaches who can help.
- New strategies or insights can be beneficial and rejuvenating.

10. **Stay Organized**

- A clutter-free environment can lead to a clutter-free mind. There is so much truth in this. I became much more productive once I got the mountain of folders out of my work area.
- Use tools and software to manage appointments, to-dos, and client information. A calendar link is one of the first things you'll need if you're just starting. Until you can figure out which CRM is best for you, I advise starting with something inexpensive and easy like Acuity for booking calls, a PayPal link to receive payment, Trello for to-dos, and a Google doc for client information. This will change as you grow, but these are free or very low cost, and you can start booking calls today.

11. Stay Connected with Your Why

- Regularly remind yourself of the reasons you chose the coaching profession. Knowing your why will keep you focused.
- This connection can reignite passion and purpose.

12. Take Regular Vacations

- It's essential to disconnect fully from work periodically, even if only for a day at a time. It's so refreshing to leave everything behind and rejuvenate.
- Whether it's a staycation or traveling, ensure you have time away from work often.

13. Limit Technology

- While technology is vital, constant notifications can be draining. (If there was a stronger word than draining, I would use it here.)
- Set specific times to check emails or messages, and try digital detoxes occasionally. There are apps in the resources section I suggest for this.

14. Develop a Morning Routine

- Start the day positively with activities that energize and center you.

- This might include reading, meditation, exercise, or any other activity that sets a positive tone for the day. I like to give my clients a productivity spreadsheet where they can fill in these times that are off-limits for any type of work.

15. Stay Hydrated and Nourished

- Drink plenty of water throughout the day. I love adding lemon to a couple of glasses daily to mix it up.
- Avoid excessive caffeine or sugar, which can lead to energy crashes.

16. Engage in Continuous Personal Growth

- Just as you encourage clients to grow, ensure you are also on a personal growth journey.
- This could be through books, courses, or personal experiences. This one isn't hard for me. I'm a learnaholic, almost to a fault.

By integrating these self-care practices, coaches can ensure they remain resilient, effective, and able to serve their clients to the best of their ability. Remember, as the saying goes, "You cannot pour from an empty cup." Taking care of oneself is paramount to taking care of others.

ETHICS IN COACHING: KEY CONSIDERATIONS

1. Confidentiality

- This goes without saying, but respect and maintain the confidentiality of all client information unless given explicit permission or legally required to disclose.

- Ensure all records, notes, and communication methods are stored securely.

2. Professional Boundaries

We touch on this a few times in this book because it's important to establish clear boundaries within the coach-client relationship. Avoid dual relationships that can impair judgment or create conflicts of interest. Many coaches and clients become friends. I have clients who have turned into friends, and though it's suggested to keep that boundary, I have been fortunate. I think we can all envision how this could become a problem. What tends to be a lot more difficult is the reverse—the friend turned client. I think that should be on a case-by-case basis, but I don't advise it overall.

Avoid any form of romantic or inappropriate personal relationship with clients. I wholeheartedly agree with this. If strong feelings emerge, it's time to cut off the coach-client relationship and nurture what you have.

3. **Competence**

- Only offer services in areas where you are trained and competent.
- Please do yourself and, more importantly, your client or prospective client a favor and recognize when a client's needs exceed your expertise and refer them to a specialist or other professional when necessary.

4. **Informed Consent**

- *Clearly* explain the coaching process, goals, methods, and associated costs, and make sure the client fully understands.
- Ensure clients are informed of their rights, including confidentiality, and obtain their explicit agreement before starting.

5. **Avoiding Harm**

- Always, always act in the best interest of your clients.
- Stay updated with best practices to ensure your clients receive effective and relevant coaching.

6. **Integrity**

- Be honest and transparent in all dealings with clients. You'll read this more than a few times in this book.

- Do not misrepresent your qualifications and expertise.

7. Cultural Competence and Sensitivity

- Understand and respect cultural differences and individual uniqueness.
- Continuously educate yourself on issues of diversity, equity, and inclusion.

8. Ongoing Professional Development

- Commit to continuous learning and professional growth.
- Engage in supervision or peer review to receive feedback and uphold ethical standards. As time goes by, we tend to be close to our businesses. Step back. Bring in a second set of eyes every year and give them the rundown of how you run your business. You'll be surprised at little nuances that pop up that could use tweaking.

9. Fees and Financial Arrangements

- Clearly communicate all fees and financial arrangements before beginning coaching.
- Avoid any potential conflicts of interest in financial dealings.

10. **Termination and Referral**

- As discussed earlier, recognize when it's appropriate to end the coaching relationship, whether due to the client's goals being met, a lack of progress, or other reasons.
- If needed, refer the client to other resources or professionals.

11. **Representation**

- Avoid making exaggerated claims or guarantees about the potential results of coaching.
- Always advertise and promote your services with honesty and integrity.

12. **Awareness of Limitations**

Understand that coaching is not therapy. If a client exhibits signs of mental health issues, refer them to an appropriate mental health professional.

13. **Addressing Ethical Concerns**

- If faced with an ethical dilemma, seek guidance from peers, supervisors, or relevant professional bodies.
- Have a process in place for addressing and resolving any ethical complaints.

14. Stay Updated with Professional Guidelines

Regularly review and stay updated with the ethical guidelines set by professional coaching organizations, like the International Coach Federation (ICF) or the Center for Credentialing and Education (CCE).

Incorporating these ethical considerations ensures coaching remains a trusted and reputable profession. Coaches need to commit to these principles not only as a professional obligation but also as a commitment to the well-being and success of their clients.

DIVERSITY, EQUITY, AND INCLUSION IN COACHING

Definition:

Diversity refers to the presence of distinct characteristics within a group, such as race, gender, age, religion, disability, sexual orientation, nationality, or other attributes. Equity ensures fair treatment, opportunities, and advancement for all, recognizing that not everyone starts at the same place. Inclusion is about creating an environment where everyone feels valued and has the opportunity to fully participate.

1. **Importance in Coaching**

   - **Diverse Perspectives:** Engaging with diverse clientele can enrich a coach's perspective, enhancing their ability to relate to and support a broader range of individuals.

   - **Relevance in a Globalized World:** As coaching becomes more global, understanding various cultural, social, and personal nuances is crucial.

   - **Building Trust:** Clients from marginalized backgrounds may have unique concerns and histories that need acknowledgment for a trusting coach-client relationship.

2. **Strategies for Promoting DEI in Coaching**

- **Continuous Learning:** Engage in training and workshops that enhance understanding of DEI issues. This includes recognizing unconscious biases and equipping oneself with the tools to address them.

- **Inclusive Marketing:** Use diverse imagery, languages, and stories in your marketing material to resonate with a broader audience.

- **Offer Sliding Scale Fees:** Recognizing economic disparities, consider implementing a sliding scale fee system to make coaching accessible to clients from various economic backgrounds.

- **Tailored Approaches:** Understand that one-size-fits-all techniques may not work for everyone. Customize your approach based on the unique backgrounds and needs of your clients.

3. **Benefits of DEI in Coaching**

- **Broader Client Base:** By being inclusive, you open your services to a larger market.

- **Richer Client Relationships:** Understanding and valuing each client's unique experiences can lead to deeper, more meaningful coach-client relationships.

- **Personal Growth:** Engaging with diverse perspectives enriches personal understanding and promotes growth as a coach and individual.

4. **Challenges and Considerations**

- **Avoid Tokenism:** Embracing DEI means genuinely understanding and valuing diversity, not just adding it for appearances. #truthbomb
- **Cultural Sensitivity:** Be aware of cultural nuances and avoid making assumptions based on stereotypes.
- **Regularly Re-Evaluate:** The world and its understanding of DEI issues evolve. Regularly review and update your DEI policies and practices to stay current.

In conclusion, embracing Diversity, Equity, and Inclusion in a coaching business is not just about being ethical or tapping into a larger market. It's about recognizing and valuing the inherent worth of every individual, regardless of their background, and ensuring they feel seen, heard, and understood in the coaching process.

CHARACTERISTICS OF GREAT LEADERSHIP

1. **Deep Listening:** The ability to genuinely hear what is being said and, perhaps more importantly, what isn't. This is foundational to understanding your client's true needs and feelings.

2. **Empathetic Understanding:** Recognizing your client's emotions and responding compassionately.

3. **Authentic Presence:** Being fully present in interactions, showing up as one's true self without pretense. Showing up means just that: Show up to your calls on time and avoid rescheduling if possible.

4. **Tactful Communication:** Conveying messages in a way that respects the client's feelings and perspective without using loud or commanding tones. Depending on the boundaries you have in place for your program, communication also means always replying to DMs and/or emails promptly, if not by you, then by your support team. There's nothing more unprofessional than ignoring messages.

5. **Intuitive Insight:** Tapping into an innate sense of understanding, often derived from reading between the lines or sensing the energy in the room.

6. **Humble Inquiry:** Asking questions from a place of genuine curiosity rather than making assumptions or judgments.

7. **Relatable Storytelling:** Sharing personal stories or experiences that can offer guidance, resonate with the client's journey, and foster deeper connections. Most people love to hear personal stories.

8. **Quiet Confidence:** Believing in oneself and one's abilities without needing constant external validation or a prominent platform.

9. **Patient Guidance:** Recognizing that growth and understanding take time and providing consistent support at the client's pace.

10. **Collaborative Spirit:** Promoting a sense of partnership where both coach and client learn from each other, emphasizing mutual respect. The coach should not command authority. The most successful coaches are honest and, at times, show their vulnerability.

11. **Reflective Practice:** Encouraging clients to reflect on their experiences, thoughts, and feelings, facilitating deeper self-awareness. Self-awareness is needed in all aspects of your life, not just coaching.

12. **Grounded Feedback:** Offering constructive feedback in a manner that is honest and supportive, ensuring it's received in the intended spirit. There are some really bad coaches out there. There's nothing worse than a coach who acts put out, belittles, or laughs at their client.

13. **Cultivating Safe Spaces:** Ensuring clients feel safe, respected, and valued in every interaction, allowing them to be vulnerable and genuine.

By embodying these skills, a coach in any specialty can lead effectively without needing to dominate conversations or center themselves in the spotlight. Their influence is derived from the genuine connections they forge and the impactful guidance they provide.

CHARACTERISTICS OF BAD LEADERSHIP

1. **Being Fake:** Giving feedback or advice that feels insincere or scripted, causing clients or team members to doubt the authenticity of the relationship. Misalignment in actions is palpable.

2. **Bullying Behavior:** Using one's position as the leader/coach to demean or belittle clients and/or team members, fostering a relationship built on fear rather than trust.

3. **Mockery in Feedback:** Turning mistakes or learning moments into a joke or ridicule, eroding the client's and/or team member's confidence and trust.

4. **Creating Inner Circles:** Cultivating an exclusive rapport with select clients or team members leaves others out of key decisions, feeling undervalued and sidelined. Engaging in behind-the-scenes discussions further erodes trust.

5. **Displaying Favoritism:** Demonstrating a preference for certain clients or team members while overlooking the aspirations and needs of others, leading to potential feelings of resentment and division.

6. **Vague Guidance:** Providing inconsistent or ambiguous feedback, making it difficult for clients or team members to understand expectations or identify areas for growth. This includes giving conflicting advice on different days or delegating

a task to one team member only to give contradictory instructions to another.

7. **Resistance to New Perspectives:** Staying stuck in one's ways with the "it's my way or the highway" mentality and dismissing your team members' fresh ideas or approaches for your business growth. Thinking your way is the only way.

8. **Lack of Empathetic Listening:** Have you ever felt like you're speaking, but no one's listening? That's how clients and team members feel when their emotions, concerns, or dreams are brushed aside. Jumping straight to solutions without truly hearing can leave them feeling unseen and undervalued.

9. **Unclear Communication:** Providing ambiguous direction and making evasive statements like, "I'll look into it" or, "Let me get back to you on that," without follow-up, leaving clients and/or team members uncertain and lacking direction.

10. **Unreliability:** Consistently missing or rescheduling sessions, often arriving late or being noticeably distracted during calls/meetings by taking calls or texting. This weakens the trust foundation and conveys a lack of respect and commitment to the client and/or team member.

Awareness of these bad leadership characteristics helps coaches cultivate a more nurturing, inclusive, and effective coaching relationship with their clients and team members.

COMMON COACHING PITFALLS AND HOW TO AVOID THEM

Coaching, like any profession, has its share of pitfalls. Here's a list of common pitfalls you might face and ways to navigate or, better yet, avoid them:

1. Not Setting Clear Boundaries

Avoidance: Set clear terms at the beginning about availability, means of communication, and the scope of your coaching services. This ensures that neither you nor your clients burn out or feel taken advantage of.

2. Avoiding Difficult Conversations

Avoidance: Coaching sometimes requires addressing sensitive topics or offering critical feedback. Instead of avoiding them, approach them with empathy, active listening, and constructive guidance.

3. Not Continuously Learning

Avoidance: The coaching industry is constantly evolving. Dedicate time for ongoing education through seminars, books, or courses. Staying updated ensures you provide the best advice to clients.

4. Becoming Too Emotionally Invested

Avoidance: While empathy is crucial in coaching, it's important to maintain some emotional distance to give objective advice. Develop self-awareness and mindfulness practices to keep personal emotions in check.

5. Over-Promising and Under-Delivering

Avoidance: Always be realistic about what you can offer. It's better to under-promise and over-deliver than the other way around.

6. Not Having a Clear Niche

Avoidance: Trying to be everything to everyone dilutes your brand and expertise. Identify and market to your niche. It establishes you as an expert in that specific area.

7. Not Seeking Feedback

Avoidance: Regularly ask for feedback from clients. It's the most direct way to understand areas of improvement and evolve as a coach.

8. Lacking a Business Strategy

Avoidance: Coaching is also a business. Have clear business goals, pricing strategies, and marketing plans in place.

9. **Ignoring Self-Care**

Avoidance: To provide the best support to others, you must take care of yourself first. Ensure you set aside time for self-care, relaxation, and personal growth.

10. **Being Over-Reliant on One Approach**

Avoidance: No two clients are the same. While having a methodology is important, be flexible and adaptable in your approach.

11. **Not Utilizing Technology**

Avoidance: Use available tech tools for scheduling, reminders, video sessions, or feedback collection to streamline processes and improve client experiences.

12. **Ignoring Group Dynamics in Group Coaching**

Avoidance: Recognize that group coaching isn't just individual coaching multiplied. Understand group dynamics, ensure everyone gets a voice, and manage potential conflicts.

13. **Neglecting Marketing and Branding**

Avoidance: Regularly update your website, use social media effectively, and network within the industry. Make sure potential clients can find and relate to you.

14. Avoiding Supervision or Peer Feedback

Avoidance: Just as therapists often have supervisors, coaches can benefit from peer feedback or supervision to maintain best practices.

15. Failing to Establish Trust

Avoidance: Always maintain confidentiality, be punctual, and truly listen. Trust is the foundation of any coaching relationship.

By being aware of these pitfalls, you can more effectively navigate your career, ensuring that you grow professionally and provide the best possible value to your clients.

TOOLS AND TECHNOLOGY FOR COACHES

As mentioned earlier, signing on with an all-in-one platform is much easier and more cost-effective. However, I'd like to give you options to bootstrap if you feel the need.

1. **Coaching Platforms**

   - **Satori:** An all-in-one business solution for coaches, offering scheduling, invoicing, and client management.
   - **CoachAccountable:** Allows coaches to set client metrics, create worksheets, and more.
   - **Nudge Coach:** A mobile-first platform useful for health and fitness coaches to track client progress.

2. **Scheduling Tools**

   - **Calendly:** An online appointment scheduling software that integrates with most calendars and offers time-zone flexibility.
   - **Acuity Scheduling:** Enables appointment bookings, cancellations, and rescheduling.

3. **Video Conferencing**

   - **Zoom:** Popular for virtual coaching sessions, webinars, and group coaching.

- **Microsoft Teams:** A business-focused communication tool that integrates with Microsoft Office products.

4. **Payment Platforms**

- **PayPal:** A widely used platform for receiving payments.
- **Stripe:** A payment gateway allowing businesses to accept payments online.
- **Square:** Useful for in-person sessions or workshops with its card reader capability.

5. **CRM (Client Relationship Management) Systems**

- **HubSpot:** Offers a free CRM along with marketing tools.
- **Zoho CRM:** Known for its customization and integration capabilities.
- **Salesforce:** A comprehensive CRM popular with larger coaching businesses.
- **FG Funnels:** An all-in-one platform I use and *love*. More information is below in the resources section.
- **MPro:** All-in-one platform.
- **Kajabi:** All-in-one platform.

6. Communication and Collaboration

- **Slack**: For communication with teams or groups, it is especially useful for group coaching programs. I love Slack.
- **Trello or Asana:** Project management tools to organize tasks, client progression, or program development. I use both and like them for different reasons.

7. Marketing and Branding

- **Canva:** A graphic design platform useful for creating marketing materials, worksheets, and other visual aids. I love this one, too.
- **Mailchimp or ConvertKit:** For email marketing, newsletters, and managing subscriber lists.

8. Feedback and Assessment

- **SurveyMonkey or Google Forms:** To gather feedback, conduct assessments, or intake new clients. I cannot even imagine my business without my Google Drive.
- **Typeform:** Creates interactive forms, quizzes, and surveys that can enhance client engagement.

9. **Learning and Course Platforms**

- **Teachable or Thinkific:** Good for offering online courses or modules as a part of your coaching program.
- **Kajabi:** An all-in-one platform for creating online courses, hosting webinars, and building client portals.
- **FG Funnels:** An all-in-one platform I use and love. More information is below in the resources section.
- **Membervault:** Free up to fifty sign-ups.

10. **Online Communities**

- **Mighty Networks or Circle:** For creating private communities or groups related to your coaching program. There are also Facebook and LinkedIn groups.

11. **Analytics and SEO**

- **Google Analytics:** To track website traffic and user behavior.
- **SEMrush or Ahrefs:** For SEO and keyword research, helping your coaching website rank higher in search results.

By leveraging these tools and technologies, coaches can ensure a seamless experience for their clients, optimize their business operations, and maintain a competitive edge in the industry. However, it's essential to continuously assess the tools' effectiveness and stay updated with emerging technologies.

THE COACH'S TOOLKIT: Tools and Techniques for Coaching Excellence

1. SWOT Analysis

Purpose: Helps clients identify their Strengths, Weaknesses, Opportunities, and Threats.

Application: Ideal for individuals starting a new venture, facing a major decision, or wanting a comprehensive personal or business analysis. I recommend revisiting this every six months and making adjustments as needed.

2. Wheel of Life

Purpose: Visual tool that allows clients to reflect on their current satisfaction levels across various life areas.

Application: Useful for holistic life coaching but also helpful with any coaching niche client.

3. Powerful Questioning

Purpose: Encourage deeper reflection and insight.

Sample Questions:

- What's holding you back?
- What does success look like for you?

- How would your life change if this issue were resolved?

4. Visualization Techniques

Purpose: Helps clients imagine a desired future, leading to increased motivation.

Application: Effective for goal setting, overcoming fears, or manifesting desires. It's used for writing excellent sales copy so the reader can feel and understand what you're saying.

5. Mind Mapping

Purpose: Brainstorming tool that visually organizes thoughts, ideas, or goals.

Application: Useful for project planning, idea generation, or understanding complex concepts.

6. Reflective Journaling

Purpose: Allows clients to record their thoughts, feelings, and insights, aiding in self-awareness.

Application: Recommended as a daily practice or following significant events or coaching sessions. It's helpful to get a full understanding when looking back at what has worked and what hasn't.

7. The GROW Model

Purpose: A structured approach to setting and achieving goals.

Goal: What does the client want?

Reality: Where is the client now?

Options: What could the client do?

Way Forward: What will the client do?

8. 360-Degree Feedback

Purpose: Collect comprehensive feedback from a client's peers, subordinates, superiors, and themselves.

Application: Vital for leadership or executive coaching to provide a rounded view of a client's impact.

9. Anchoring

Purpose: Technique from NLP (Neuro-Linguistic Programming) where a certain gesture, touch, or action is linked to a specific emotion or feeling.

Application: Useful for invoking positive states or combatting anxiety.

10. **Values Assessment**

Purpose: Helps clients identify their core values.

Application: Assists in decision-making, understanding motivations, or when feeling conflicted.

11. **Role Play**

Purpose: Allows clients to practice conversations, confrontations, or scenarios in a safe environment.

Application: Effective for preparing for difficult conversations, interviews, or understanding others' perspectives.

12. **Feedback Loop Creation**

Purpose: Establish a system for clients to receive ongoing feedback about their actions and progress.

Application: Essential for continuous improvement and aligning actions with goals.

FINANCIAL MANAGEMENT FOR COACHES

1. Budgeting and Forecasting

Establish a Budget: Outline expected income, fixed costs (like platform subscriptions, office space, and professional memberships), and variable costs.

Regularly Forecast: Periodically update your financial forecasts based on actual business performance.

2. Pricing Strategy

Know Your Worth: Understand the value you bring and set prices that reflect your expertise, experience, and the market demand.

Flexible Pricing: Consider offering package deals, retainer agreements, or tiered pricing based on client needs.

3. Separate Business and Personal Finances

Open a separate business bank account. This keeps financial records clean and makes tax time easier.

4. Savings and Emergency Fund

Allocate a percentage of your income to a business savings account for unforeseen expenses or slower business periods.

5. Invest in Continuous Education

Allocate funds for professional development. This not only improves your skills but can also justify higher rates.

6. Tax Planning

- **Understand Deductibles:** Know what business expenses can be written off to reduce taxable income.
- **Quarterly Estimates:** If applicable in your country, make quarterly tax payments to avoid year-end surprises.
- **Seek Expertise:** Consider hiring an accountant or using software like QuickBooks, FreshBooks, or Xero to manage business finances.

7. Manage Cash Flow

- Monitor income and expenses regularly to ensure you have a positive cash flow.
- Consider using invoicing and accounting tools to help with timely billing and collections.

8. Insurance

Consider getting liability insurance, especially if you're dealing with areas that may have higher risks.

9. **Retirement Planning**

Think long-term by investing in retirement accounts suitable for self-employed individuals or business owners.

10. **Debt Management**

If you've taken out loans or have business credit cards, create a strategy to effectively manage and pay down that debt.

11. **Financial Review and Analysis**

- Regularly review your financial statements. Tools like profit and loss statements will provide insights into the health of your business.
- Adjust strategies based on financial performance.

12. **Expand Revenue Streams**

Look for additional ways to monetize your expertise, such as online courses, e-books, group coaching, or workshops.

Effective financial management ensures the sustainability of your coaching practice. It's crucial to stay educated about financial best practices, regularly review your financial health, and seek expert advice when needed.

LEGAL ASPECTS FOR COACHES

1. Coaching Agreements/Contracts

Scope of Work: Clearly define the services to be provided and the coaching sessions' duration, frequency, and format.

Confidentiality: Address how client information will be treated and maintained.

Payment Terms: Specify payment amounts, due dates, and methods. Address refund policies if applicable.

Termination Clause: Outline circumstances under which either party can terminate the agreement and any associated terms.

2. Licensing and Certification

While coaching isn't regulated in the same way as professions like counseling or therapy, certain areas or niches might require specific certifications or adherence to established standards, such as those set by the International Coach Federation (ICF).

3. Confidentiality

- Maintaining client confidentiality is crucial. It's not just good practice; it's a legal obligation in many jurisdictions.

- Be aware of exceptions where disclosure might be necessary, such as harm to self or others.

4. Insurance

Professional Liability Insurance: This protects coaches from potential legal claims regarding their advice or guidance.

General Liability Insurance: For those who operate in a physical space, this covers accidents or injuries that might occur during sessions.

5. Business Structure

Determine the best legal structure for your coaching business, such as sole proprietorship, LLC, or corporation. Each has its benefits and considerations regarding liability, taxation, and management.

6. Intellectual Property

Protect your coaching materials, methods, and unique products or services through copyright, trademarks, or patents where applicable.

7. Data Protection and Privacy

- Be aware of regulations, such as the General Data Protection Regulation (GDPR) in the European Union, that dictate how personal data should be collected, stored, and processed.

- If you have one, ensure your website complies with privacy laws, and consider including a privacy policy detailing how client data is used.

8. Boundary Setting

There are many reasons boundary setting is crucial. Clearly define the coach-client relationship. Knowing where coaching ends and where therapy or other professional services might begin is essential. Overstepping can result in legal complications.

9. Advertising and Marketing

Ensure that your promotional materials, testimonials, and claims are accurate and don't mislead potential clients.

10. Local, State, and International Regulations

There may be specific legal considerations depending on where you and your clients are located. If you're coaching clients internationally, be aware of and adhere to the regulations in your and your client's countries.

It's always advisable for coaches to seek legal counsel in their jurisdiction to ensure they are aware of all pertinent regulations and requirements. Regular reviews and updates of contracts and practices will help maintain compliance and foster client trust.

MARKET-SPECIFIC TIPS AND INSIGHTS: How coaching differs in various parts of the world

Specific advice for major markets (at the time of this publication):

1. **North America (USA and Canada)**

Market: Highly competitive but also the largest in revenue and number of coaches.

Key Insight: Certification is highly valued. Local bodies like the International Coach Federation (ICF) are recognized, and credentials from such organizations can greatly enhance credibility.

2. **Europe (UK, Germany, France)**

Market: Mature market with a strong emphasis on executive and leadership coaching.

Key Insight: Cultural nuances, like the German emphasis on privacy or the UK's respect for traditional institutions, play into the coaching dynamic.

Tip: Understand the specific cultural nuances of each country. For example, in Germany, being direct and precise might be appreciated, whereas, in the UK, a more relationship-driven approach might be preferred.

3. Asia (India, China, Japan)

Market: Rapidly growing, especially in urban centers. However, coaching is often confused with mentoring or consulting.

Key Insight: Saving face is significant in many Asian cultures. Direct feedback or confrontation could be counterproductive.

Tip: Establish credibility. In countries like India and China, where coaching is a newer industry, credentials, testimonials, and proven track records can be vital. In Japan, respect for hierarchy and seniority is essential, so understanding corporate dynamics is crucial.

4. Latin America (Brazil, Mexico)

Market: Emergent, with a growing appreciation for personal development and organizational growth.

Key Insight: Family and personal relationships strongly influence business and decision-making processes.

Tip: Networking is key. Building personal relationships can lead to business opportunities. Also, understanding the significance of local events, festivals, and cultural nuances can aid in rapport building.

5. Middle East (UAE, Saudi Arabia)

Market: Niche but growing, especially in global hubs like Dubai.

Key Insight: The importance of local customs and traditions, such as the separation of genders in certain settings, can't be ignored.

Tip: Culturally sensitive coaching is essential. Understanding local customs, religious practices, and societal norms can help offer relevant coaching strategies.

6. Africa (South Africa, Nigeria)

Market: Still nascent but with a lot of potential, especially in urban hubs.

Key Insight: There's a strong community and collectivist culture in many African societies, which contrasts with the individualistic approach seen in Western coaching models.

Tip: Group coaching or workshops might be more effective than one-on-one sessions in certain settings. Leveraging local networks and community leaders can be a strategic move.

Across all regions, it's crucial to approach coaching with an open mind, ready to adapt and learn from every individual and culture. By being culturally sensitive and adaptable, a coach can make meaningful connections and offer valuable insights, irrespective of geographical boundaries.

TOP 10 COACHING NICHES

1. Life Coach
2. Career Coach
3. Sales Coach
4. Business Coach
5. Health Coach
6. Leadership Coach
7. Wellness Coach
8. Sex Coach
9. Nutrition Coach
10. Money Coach

FASCINATING COACHING STATS

The estimated global market value from coaching is well over $15.2 billion, with an estimated 93,000 coaches (2023), and is rapidly expanding, according to Forbes.com.

Business Coaching Impact: A study by the ICF found that 86% of companies that invested in coaching for their employees saw a positive return on investment (ROI), with benefits such as improved teamwork, increased productivity, and better employee morale.

Client Satisfaction: Client satisfaction with coaching is high. According to a survey by the ICF, 99% of clients who had experienced coaching were satisfied with their coaching experience, with 96% stating they would repeat the process.

Impact on Well-being: Coaching can have a positive impact on individuals' well-being. A study published in the International Journal of Evidence Based Coaching and Mentoring found that coaching interventions were associated with improvements in self-esteem, self-efficacy, and psychological well-being.

Cross-Cultural Coaching: With globalization, cross-cultural coaching has gained prominence. In a global coaching survey, 81% of coaches reported working with clients from different cultural backgrounds, highlighting the importance of cultural competence in coaching.

POTENTIAL FUTURE TRENDS IN COACHING (2024-2034)

1. Integration of Advanced Technologies

As technologies like AI and virtual reality (VR) become more accessible, we'll see a shift in how coaching is delivered. Imagine a coaching session where the client is immersed in a VR environment designed to support their growth or AI-powered tools providing instant feedback during training exercises.

2. Holistic Coaching Models

Moving away from niche specializations, there will be a surge in holistic coaching models that address the complete human experience, integrating physical, emotional, mental, and spiritual dimensions.

3. Increased Focus on Mental Health

With growing awareness about mental health, coaches will integrate principles from psychology and therapy, making sessions more about holistic well-being than professional growth.

4. Micro-Coaching Sessions

The age of bite-sized content (like TikTok or Twitter) will influence coaching, leading to the popularity of short, focused coaching sessions addressing specific issues.

5. Group and Community Coaching

Individual coaching will always have its place, but there will be a rise in group coaching sessions and community-driven platforms where peers support and learn from each other.

6. Globalization and Diverse Clientele

As the world becomes more interconnected, coaches will work with clients from diverse cultural backgrounds, demanding an understanding of global perspectives and cultural sensitivities.

7. Personal Branding for Coaches

With the rise of social media influencers, coaches will increasingly focus on personal branding, leveraging platforms like Instagram, YouTube, and podcasts to reach and engage with potential clients.

8. Sustainability and Social Impact Coaching

As businesses aim to be more sustainable and socially responsible, there will be a growing need for coaches specializing in guiding businesses toward these goals.

9. Lifelong Learning and Upgradation

The rapid pace of change in today's world means coaches must commit to lifelong learning, regularly updating their skills and methodologies.

10. Ethics and Regulation

As coaching becomes even more mainstream, there will likely be more standardized regulations, certifications, and ethical guidelines governing the profession.

11. Hybrid Coaching Models

A mix of online and offline sessions allows for both the convenience of remote coaching and the personal touch of face-to-face interactions.

12. Neuroscience-Backed Techniques

With advances in our understanding of the brain, expect techniques grounded in neuroscience to validate and enhance coaching strategies.

By staying ahead of these trends, you can ensure you're offering your clients the best, most relevant services and staying competitive in a quickly evolving industry.

ORGANIC VISIBILITY AND TRAFFIC IDEAS

Buynow.io: One click. Create products from your images, post, and share. Also provides landing pages, running ads, being an affiliate, and more. https://buynow.io/docs?type=d01&lunk=buynow_home

Collaborate in an online giveaway to build your email list. Remember, your email is gold. It's yours. Your social media following can disappear tomorrow.

Collaboration Station: Join to find like-minded creators for joint webinars, bundles, summits, and podcasts, not to mention all the best affiliate resources.

https://www.collaborationstation.co/?a_aid=karajames

Host an online giveaway.

Promote in Facebook groups: Here's a huge list of Facebook Groups where you can promote. https://docs.google.com/spreadsheets/d/1t-D2I7ZMCK7vaiPO23lrNX9PdYPtNc-Le_M5aOyzMt6o/edit

Do Instagram reels, carousels, and stories.

Join LinkedIn: Connect and DM.

Join LinkedIn Groups and post in those groups. (Some of these groups have hundreds of thousands of people.)

Create your own LinkedIn Group.

Create a LinkedIn Page and then fill out an application with LinkedIn to go live once you've reached 150 connections on the page and have steady, original, and engaged posts.

Create a blog. Make sure it's SEO optimized.

Guest blog for others and allow it on your site.

Create and share personalized swag in minutes www.buynow.io

Create an affiliate program and share it with your list. This gives a huge incentive for them to sell your product or service. https://www.firstpromoter.com/

Participate in or host a summit. To find out if you're eligible to participate in summits related to your niche, email kimberly@entrepreneursrocketfuel.com.

Ask to be interviewed on a podcast or create a podcast.

Get the latest podcasting, blogging, and marketing opportunities at https://weeklyrocket. theaudaciousagency.com/

In Your Facebook group: Offer gamification or host a three or five-day challenge.

Write a book. Reach out to Chris at chris@jetlaunch.net

Be the President of PIVOT Magazine for your city: https://www.pivotmagazines.com/

Get the ultimate visibility package: Includes your radio show, podcast, bestselling book, TV show, course, magazine article, TEDx talk, and speaker training. https://www.jetlaunchpublishing.com/

Publish a book on Kindle.

Clubhouse: Join, create a room, and speak.

Resend the unopened emails announcing your offer with a different subject line.

Use an abandoned cart email strategy to recover lost leads.

Join Pinterest, the world's third-largest search engine. Get a business account and create pins.

Make your business searchable. Get a Google My Business account. Create posts and get reviews.

Create a YouTube channel.

Host a virtual workshop. Introduce them to one piece of your offer for a low price ($27-47 for one to three hours). At the end, invite them to your core offer.

Host an in-person workshop. (Same as above, but charge $97 and offer light refreshments.)

Host a VIP day: A hands-on day with you getting work done. Also include swag and a workbook.

Host an in-person high-ticket retreat at a beautiful hotel or location. This would be a high-ticket offer (ranging from $1997-$50k) where you work with an intimate group of your clients for a weekend or a week. This can include meals, swag, a beautiful workbook, and possibly one or more of the following: dinner together, fun outings, massage, yoga, etc., depending on your area of expertise. Reach out if you'd like more info.

Create affiliate links for your products: https://www. firstpromoter.com/

Slideshare: Upload free Slide decks to share at https:// www.slideshare.net/

Answer Questions on www.quora.com to show you're the expert and gain followers.

Quuu: Get relevant people to share your content with their audience at https://quuu.co/

JV partnerships: https://www.jvzoo.com/

Publish a free course on Udemy: https://www. udemy.com/

Sign up for HARO (Help A Reporter Out). Bloggers connect with journalists to tell their stories. HARO distributes more than 50,000 highly respected journalists. https://www.helpareporter.com/

Participate in forums.

Meetup: Host events targeted to your ideal clients. https://www.meetup.com/home/

Free publicity for expert sources: https://www. sourcebottle.com

Tell your story at www.medium.com

Additional Helpful Resources for Business Growth, Time Management, and Your Client's Success

Opt-intelligence.com: Get leads without landing pages (no lead magnet needed).

Beacon: Create and share lead magnets at https://beacon.by/

Collect video testimonials from those who have worked with you in any capacity. https://www.videopeel.com/

Skitch app: for screenshots of testimonials and positive feedback.

Testimonials: https://testimonial.to/

Swag: Purchase your logoed swag to give to your clients or sell.

- **Sponsor events with Swag or donate it.**
- **4Imprint:** https://www.4imprint.com/?mkid =34i_01_004&s_kwcid=AL!4167!10! 74011121535833!123801982&utm_ source=bing&utm_medium=cpc&utm_ term=4imprint&utm_campaign= 4imprint%20Bing&ef_id=9e61478a 574e1ead210227669e782b4f:G:s

- **Printed Mint:** https://printedmint.com/
- **Printify:** https://printify.com/cpc_it_selling_made_simple/?utm_source=salsa&utm_medium=cpc&utm_campaign=salsa_v1&salsa_clickid=86470904621

Send a personalized note using https://www.handwrytten.com/

Brand Archetype: https://www.brandarchetypequiz.com/

Branding Colors: www.coolors.co
https://www.color-hex.com/

Transcribe Your Videos

- **Otter:** https://otter.ai/login
- **Temi:** https://www.temi.com/
- **Rev:** https://www.rev.com/
- **Verbit:** https://get.verbit.ai/ppv-live-transcription-captions/?utm_source=propelmedia&utm_medium=PPV&utm_campaign=12442495&utm_term=240876&utm_content=7563d7d-7458254b66ed1e3ccce8a72dd

HELPFUL COURSES FROM PRODUCTIVITY TO PR

Authentic Genius One Year Program: Amazing PR opportunities to elevate your brand and take it to the next level with monthly business consulting and unique positioning for you and your company through multiple PR channels, including radio/podcast, TEDx, book signing, TV, print, social media, and more. https://drjulieducharme.com/www.shelbyjolong.com

Banish business clutter. Digital Clutter Cure ($597) is an online program designed to eliminate overwhelm, ditch the digital and physical clutter, and transform your business with streamlined systems that increase clarity, productivity, and profits.

https://www.banishbusinessclutter.com/a/24508/NhxJgESX

Get Productive with G-Suite (now Google Workspace): A $37 course with a step-by-step framework that allows you to take action, fitting Google's Suite of Products *(free or paid)* together for ultimate productivity. The course includes modules related to Google My Business and Gmail Inbox Zero and the top 40 time-saving Google hacks.

https://pursueandthrive--withdara.thrivecart.com/gpg37/

Last Pass Mastery: LastPass Mastery ($47) is a mini course helping you make the most out of keeping your password sharing safe and much more. https://pursue-andthrive--withdara.thrivecart.com/lastpassmastery/

Maximize Your Mac: This easy-to-follow roadmap shows you how to set up, organize, and simplify everything you do on your Mac. It is normally $197, but get it for $97 using coupon code 100off. https://www.banishbusinessclutter.com/offers/2Qta9dFB/checkout?coupon_code=100OFF

BOOK RECOMMENDATIONS

- *She Leads in Her Truth: The 7 Cornerstones of Authentic & Confident Female Leadership for Women CEOs, Managers, & Entrepreneurs* by Camille Hale
- *The Power of 10: Rapid Revenue Strategies* by Jason Miller and the Strategic Advisor Board
- *The Power of 10 Reloaded: Rapid Revenue Strategies for Business* by Jason Miller and SAB
- *Rocket Fuel* by Wickman and Winters
- *Free to Focus* by Michael Hyatt
- *Automate & Grow* by Michael Devellano
- *Building A Story Brand* by Donald Miller
- *Start with Why* by Simon Sinek
- *Resonate: Present Visual Stories that Transform Audiences* by Nancy Duarte
- *Blue Ocean Strategy* by Roger Wayne, W. Chan Kim, et al.
- *Psycho-Cybernetics* by Maxwell Maltz
- *Mindset* by Carol Dweck
- *Credibility Nation* by Mitchell Levy
- *The Big Leap* by Gay Hendricks
- *I See Your Genius* by Shelby Jo Long
- *Leadership and Self-Deception* by The Arbinger Institute
- *The Brand Gap* by Marty Neumeier
- *Unstoppable Referrals* by Steve Gordon

- *Supercoach* by Michael Neill
- *Zag: The Number One Strategy of High-Performance Brands* by Marty Neumeir
- *Group Coaching: A Comprehensive Blueprint* by Ginger Cockerham
- *The Silva Mind Control Method* by Jose Silva et al.
- *Miracle Morning* by Hal Elrod
- *Leadership and Self Deception: Getting Out of the Box* by The Arbinger Institute
- *The 7 Habits of Highly Effective People: Powerful Lessons in Personal Change* by Stephen R. Covey

HELPFUL RESOURCES

Disclosure: Some of the links provided in this article may be affiliate links. This means I may earn a small commission if you purchase through one of these links. There is no additional cost to you, and I only recommend products and services that I believe are valuable and trustworthy.

The Ad Network: Advertising platform with significantly lower costs and more visibility than the competition (FB, Google, LinkedIn).
https://www.proshark.com/ref-ad-network-webinar?via=https://www.proshark.com/ref-ad-network?via=kara

Sharing the Credit: Support your favorite charity. We take the portion of your credit/debit card merchant fees you were paying to the bank and give it to your charity of choice instead.
https://saving.sharingthecredit.com/KaraJames

SAB Marketplace: Sell your programs at https://www.strategicadvisorboard.com/marketplace

Iconic Femme: https://www.iconicfemme.com/

Portfolio: https://www.iconicfemme.com/clients

StartupWeekend.org: Form of a startup team and network.

InternAvenue.com: Find internships and interns.

InternQueen.com: Pay a small fee to have an intern work for you in your business.

Acadium.com: Connects marketing students with professionals for a twelve-week apprenticeship. Charge a small fee to have a marketing student work for you for twelve weeks.

Workaholics4hire.com: Outsourcing services and project management.

AoV.com: Virtual staffing, online marketing support.

Fiverr.com: Freelancing services for as little as $5.

BestJobs.ph: Search thousands of jobs in the Philippines and abroad.

OnlineJobs.ph: Very reasonable fees. Philipino virtual assistants for all of your coaching needs. https://bit.ly/3r60nuM

HireMyMom.com: Offer a micro job.

Growthgeeks.com: Marketplace for marketing services.

Designcrowd.com: Amazing logo, web, and graphic design.

99designs.com: Logo design, web design, and other design contests.

Textbroker.com: Professional content writers for a variety of content.

Livescribe.com: Transfer writing to your computer.

ListSwapper.com: Grow your list and create joint ventures.

Warriorforum.com /warrior-joint-ventures: Establish joint ventures or partners.

RescueTime (Android, iOS, Linux, macOS, Web, Windows): A way to block distracting sites while keeping track of productivity.

Hocus Focus: A way to focus on one window at a time while blocking the rest of your tabs.

Brain.fm: Soundtracks to heighten your focusing abilities.

AirTable: This is designed to be a database, spreadsheet, and project management app to let you combine your data while creating views and images to show data on your project.

Evernote: An app to help manage your projects by organizing and cleaning out your notebooks creating master lists and project notes while adding shortcuts. This creates a workspace for tracking ideas and projects while monitoring your tasks.

Slack: An app to help you manage how much time a task can be delayed to not affect the deadlines of subsequent tasks or final projects. It's great for communicating with your clients and team members. It keeps all conversations under one channel.

Copytalk: Dictation service you can use to transcribe your recordings of conferences and events.

Otter.ai: Records and takes notes in real-time conversations or meetings.

Invideo.io: Adds music to the beginning and end of your videos.

Sanebox: An email management software that filters messages within your email that are considered unimportant and filtered into a folder.

Drift: Combines live chat, video, email, and automation as a marketing platform primarily based on conversational approaches.

Logaster: Online logo maker and generator.

Copy Paste Character: You can copy and paste free symbols, emoji, and character icons into your documents.

1001 Free Fonts: Free fonts, sortable by style.

Pixabay: Royalty-free stock photos and videos.

Unsplash: Free stock photos.

GIMP: Image editor.

Paint.NET: Free image and photo editing software for PCs.

Pixlr: Free Photoshop/photo editor.

SumoPaint: Online image editor that works in your browser.

VSCO Cam: A photography app and photo editor with stunning filters. (it's often referred to as "the Instagram for photographers.")

Tawk.to: Free messaging app that lets you monitor and chat with visitors on your website.

Batch: Send push notifications at scale.

Cyfe: An all-in-one business dashboard that lets you monitor all your business data from one place.

HelpScout: Customer Service interaction software designed for an optimal customer experience.

HelpScout Blog: Articles on customer loyalty best practices with many actionable tips.

Wufoo: Online forms and surveys.

About.me: A one-page personal website, great for your bio, can be created quickly.

SumoMe List Builder: Convert website visitors right before they're about to leave your website.

Bit.ly: Shorten custom links.

Disqus: The world's most popular comment system for your blog.

CoSchedule Headline Analyzer: This free blog post headline analyzer will score your overall headline quality and rate its ability to result in social shares, increased traffic, and SEO value.

Free PDF Creator: Create PDF documents from any Windows program, including Word, Excel, and PowerPoint.

Free Summarizer: Summarizes any text in just a few seconds, then sends you the summary via email.

iBooks Author: Creates and publishes books for iPad and Mac.

World Data Email Resources: Exclusive, free marketing content and tools, including insightful tips, tricks, and industry statistics.

Grammarly: Instantly fixes copy errors.

Hemingway: Shortens long copy. Make your writing crisp and clear.

ZenPen: Distraction-free writing zone.

Audacity: Multitrack audio recorder and editor.

Vimeo: High-quality tools for hosting, sharing, and streaming videos in gorgeous HD and 4K with no ads.

4Over4: 300 free full-color glossy business cards.

Meetup: Organize or attend local groups that get together for face-to-face events.

Loom: Great for teaching and training by creating shareable videos.

RealTimeBoard: Online whiteboard that helps you visually organize your work.

TripIt: Consolidates travel plans into a single master itinerary that can be accessed at any time and on any device, regardless of the website used to buy the ticket.

Zapier: Automate tasks between web apps (i.e., create Trello cards out of emails or PayPal payments into to-do lists).

Tomato Timer: An online timer inspired by the popular Pomodoro Technique productivity system.

Timeneye: Time tracking software for teams and freelancers.

1Password: Save your passwords and log in to sites with a single click.

LastPass: LastPass remembers all your passwords, and you can share them safely with anyone.

Momentum: When you open a new tab in Chrome, this personal dashboard pops up to help you minimize distractions and increase focus.

Noisli: Plays different sounds to calm your nerves and inspire you to write.

SelfControl: Free Mac app that lets you block access to distracting websites for a set period.

Unroll.me: Instantly see a list of all your subscription emails. Unsubscribe easily from those that no longer serve you.

Apps to Block/Limit Social Media: Freedom, Offtime, Moment, BlockSite

Time Management/Focus: FocusKeeper app for task batching (Pomodoro technique)

DocuSign: Send, sign, and approve documents from anywhere.

HelloSign: Legally binding electronic signatures.

Zoho: File management tool that lets you store files securely, share with friends, and sync across all your devices.

AppSumo: Daily software deals for entrepreneurs. Great prices and most are a one-time payment.

Project Gutenberg: Thousands of free eBooks.

Mycolorspace.com: Enter one of your branding color hex codes, and it will pull up a dozen color palettes that match it.

Sourcebottle.com is a global publicity platform that disrupts the traditional media relations model and ensures everyone has free access to media leads to tell their story.

Conversation.ai: Have a robot named Jarvis write your emails.

5minutemarketingmakeover.com: Clarify your message to grow your business. Based on the best-selling book *Building A Story Brand* by Donald Miller.

Spamanalyse.com: Spamanalyse is an app that checks your copy to make sure it's spam filter friendly.

Trustpilot: This is a great tool when asking for testimonials. You can also read reviews of other businesses.

FG Funnels (Funnel Gorgeous Funnels): Join FG Funnels all-in-one platform and receive free access to gorgeous funnel templates. They are the lowest price for all-in-one CRM (website, email, SMS, CRM, invoices, funnels and funnel templates) https://www.fgfunnels. com/join?fpr=kara73

FG Funnels Beautiful Wholesale Funnel and Slide Templates: https://www.funnelgorgeous.com/ wholesale-order-form?_ga=2.116882118.1112345326. 1632703304-223948725.1632446862

Online jobs.ph: Hire amazing VAs for a very low price. https://bit.ly/3r60nuM

Legal Coaching Contracts: Get all your legal coaching contracts in one place. https://artfulcontracts. com/?ref=1ch82hx51t

Deadline Funnel: Set up automated funnels that have deadlines. https://deadlinefunnel. com?via=101238-kara-james

FREE RESOURCES WE OFFER:

Unique Offer Ideas: https://pursueandthrive.com/unique-offer-ideas-workbook877784

Ten Common Messaging Mistakes: https://pursueandthrive.com/10-common-messaging-mistakes

The Ultimate Guide for Coaches: https://pursueandthrive.com/Ultimate-Guide-For-Coaches

JOURNEY HIGHER: ELEVATE TO YOUR NEXT LEVEL OF ELITE COACHING MASTERY

The insights and strategies in this book form the foundation. To learn everything you need to go from startup to scaling, including creating different tiered offers to fill your value ladder and ensure consistent income, join me in:

The Elite Entrepreneur

Embrace a transformative year meticulously shaped to amplify your coaching status and personally ensure consistent revenue. This program will take you from startup to successfully scaling with ease.

You will become THE only choice in your field.

Click below to learn more about this incredible one-on-one, twelve-month hybrid experience: https://pursueandthrive.com/elite-entrepreneur

If you're fueled by ambition to elevate and distinctively position your coaching brand as THE go-to expert in your field, The Elite Entrepreneur hybrid coaching is more than just a coaching program; it's your compass—your North Star—guiding you toward unparalleled coaching mastery. Dive in and get started today.

While the journey to coaching excellence involves mastering many strategies and processes, it's equally about personal evolution. You'll want to keep growing, learning, and, most importantly, stay true to your authentic self. The impact you wish to create in others begins with the changes you embrace within, and together, we position you as the leader you were meant to be.

FOLLOW US

JOIN OUR FACEBOOK GROUPS

Coach's Consultants and Service Providers Success Community

https://www.facebook.com/groups/successfulbiz women/

The USA Influencer Community

https://www.facebook.com/groups/3167252394 64776/

FREE WORKBOOK OFFER

For your complimentary workbook that will help you dive deeper and effectively implement what you've learned in this book, simply email us at:

ask@pursueanthrive.com

Please use "Coach's Blueprint Workbook" as the subject line.

"In the coaching world, authenticity is the compass that points directly to impact."

~ Kara James